NHibernate 3
Beginner's Guide

Rapidly retrieve data from your database into .NET objects

Dr. Gabriel Nicolas Schenker

Aaron Cure

PACKT PUBLISHING

open source *
community experience distilled

BIRMINGHAM - MUMBAI

NHibernate 3
Beginner's Guide

Copyright © 2011 Packt Publishing

All rights reserved. No part of this book may be reproduced, stored in a retrieval system, or transmitted in any form or by any means, without the prior written permission of the publisher, except in the case of brief quotations embedded in critical articles or reviews.

Every effort has been made in the preparation of this book to ensure the accuracy of the information presented. However, the information contained in this book is sold without warranty, either express or implied. Neither the authors, nor Packt Publishing, and its dealers and distributors will be held liable for any damages caused or alleged to be caused directly or indirectly by this book.

Packt Publishing has endeavored to provide trademark information about all of the companies and products mentioned in this book by the appropriate use of capitals. However, Packt Publishing cannot guarantee the accuracy of this information.

First published: May 2010

Second edition: August 2011

Production Reference: 1180811

Published by Packt Publishing Ltd.
Livery Place
35 Livery Street
Birmingham B3 2PB, UK

ISBN 978-1-849516-02-0

www.packtpub.com

Cover Image by Vinayak Chittar (vinayak.chittar@gmail.com)

Credits

Authors
Dr. Gabriel Nicolas Schenker
Aaron Cure

Reviewers
Fabio Maulo
José F. Romaniello

Acquisition Editor
Usha Iyer

Development Editor
Neha Mallik

Technical Editors
Llewellyn F. Rozario
Conrad Sardinha

Copy Editors
Leonard D'Silva
Kriti Sharma

Project Coordinator
Michelle Quadros

Proofreaders
Kelly Hutchinson
Aaron Nash

Indexer
Tejal Daruwale

Production Coordinators
Arvindkumar Gupta
Melwyn D'sa
Nilesh R. Mohite

Cover Work
Arvindkumar Gupta

About the Authors

Dr. Gabriel Nicolas Schenker started his career as a physicist. Following his passion and interest in stars and the universe, he chose to write his PhD thesis in astrophysics. Soon after this, he dedicated all his time to his second passion, writing and architecting software. Gabriel has since been working for over 12 years as an independent consultant, trainer, and mentor, mainly on the .NET platform. He is currently working as a chief software architect in a mid-size US company based in Austin TX, providing software and services to the pharmaceutical industry, as well as to many well-known hospitals and universities throughout the US and in many other countries around the world. Gabriel is passionate about software development and tries to make life for developers easier by providing guidelines and frameworks to reduce friction in the software development process.

He has used NHibernate in many different commercial projects, web-based, as well as Windows-based solutions. Gabriel has written many articles and blog posts about different aspects of NHibernate. He is the author behind the well-known NHibernate FAQ blog. Gabriel has also been a reviewer for the bestselling book NHibernate 3 Cookbook.

Gabriel is married and a father of four children and during his spare time likes hiking in the mountains, cooking, and reading.

> I would like to thank my lovely wife, Lydia, for supporting and encouraging me to write this book.

Aaron Cure is an avid developer, instructor, and innovator. During his 10 years in the military as a linguist and a satellite communications repair technician, he learned that his real love was computer programming.

After various throes with PHP, Classic ASP, VB, and a brief encounter with Java/JSP, he found a real passion for the .NET framework. After searching for a "better way" to carry out database storage and retrieval, Aaron stumbled across the NHibernate framework.

Unsatisfied with the options for interacting with this great framework, he founded the NHibernate Generation project (nhib-gen) on SourceForge to reduce the "barrier to entry" for most developers.

Aaron and his family run a small consulting and web hosting company doing web design and custom software development for various organizations across the country. One of their more interesting projects has been software to control laser cutting machines.

In his spare time, he also enjoys developing projects with his daughters, using everything from Lego NXT (using C# and Bluetooth communications) to the Microchip PIC platform (using JAL and USB). He also collects and restores classic farm tractors, engines, and farm equipment, as well as semi trucks and trailers. He and his family display them at tractor shows, parades, schools, and various other community events.

> This book is dedicated to my beautiful and talented wife, Sherry, and my two wonderful daughters, Kaitlyn and MacKenzie. Without their love and support, this book would have never been written. I would also like to thank my parents, Karen and Chuck, as I wouldn't be here without them.
>
> Special thanks to my editors at Packt Publishing, who had more patience with me than I think I would have had and stuck with me throughout.

About the Reviewers

Fabio Maulo has lived his youth in Montecosaro, a small village in the hills of the Marche in Italy. His first computer was a Mac128 in 1984; since then, he has always followed technology of the moment, trying to learn as much as possible. Since the end of the last century, he has been following the evolution of ORM, at first in Delphi's world and then the .NET's world. He joined NHibernate's team in 2007 and has led the project since 2008.

> Thanks to my wife and my daughter who bears my work.

José Fernando Romaniello is a senior developer with 10 years of experience in Microsoft technologies. He currently lives in Argentina and works for Tellago. José has a strong involvement in various open source projects in .NET world, and he actively contributes to uNhAddins, LinqSpecs, and HqlAddin. He enjoys sharing his knowledge in his blog as well as on mailing lists.

In 2011, he was appointed as Microsoft Most Valuable Professional in C# by Microsoft.

> I want to thank my beloved wife and my daughter; I couldn't be here without their help.

www.PacktPub.com

Support files, eBooks, discount offers and more

You might want to visit www.PacktPub.com for support files and downloads related to your book.

Did you know that Packt offers eBook versions of every book published, with PDF and ePub files available? You can upgrade to the eBook version at www.PacktPub.com and as a print book customer, you are entitled to a discount on the eBook copy. Get in touch with us at service@packtpub.com for more details.

At www.PacktPub.com, you can also read a collection of free technical articles, sign up for a range of free newsletters and receive exclusive discounts and offers on Packt books and eBooks.

PACKTLIB®

http://PacktLib.PacktPub.com

Do you need instant solutions to your IT questions? PacktLib is Packt's online digital book library. Here, you can access, read and search across Packt's entire library of books.

Why Subscribe?

- Fully searchable across every book published by Packt
- Copy and paste, print and bookmark content
- On demand and accessible via web browser

Free Access for Packt account holders

If you have an account with Packt at www.PacktPub.com, you can use this to access PacktLib today and view nine entirely free books. Simply use your login credentials for immediate access.

Table of Contents

Preface	1
Chapter 1: First Look	**7**
What is NHibernate	7
What is new in NHibernate 3.0	8
Why would I use it	9
Where do I get it	10
Is there documentation available	11
Can I get help using NHibernate	12
Is there commercial support available	13
Who uses it	13
Summary	14
Chapter 2: A First Complete Sample	**15**
Prepare our development environment	15
Defining a model	20
Time for action – Creating the product inventory model	20
Mapping our model	22
Time for action – Creating the mapping classes	23
Creating the database schema	25
Time for action – Creating the database	26
Creating a session factory	30
Time for action – Creating a session factory	30
Opening a session	32
Time for action – Opening a session to the database	32
Persisting objects to the database	33
Time for action – Adding a new category to the database	34
Reading from the database	36
Time for action – Loading the list of all categories from the database	36
Doing the same without NHibernate – using ADO.NET only	38
Summary	39

Table of Contents

Chapter 3: Creating a Model   41
What is a model   41
Model first versus data first   42
Elements of a model   43
    Entity   43
    Value object   44
Time for action – Creating a Name value object   45
Creating an entity   47
Time for action – Creating a base entity   48
Time for action – Creating a Customer entity   50
Defining relations between entities   52
    Owns or contains   52
    One-to-many   53
    One-to-one   54
    Many-to-many   55
The order entry model   56
Time for action – Implementing an order entry model   56
Summary   62

Chapter 4: Defining the Database Schema   63
What is a database schema   63
    Who owns the database   64
Time for action – Creating the OrderingSystem database   64
Laying the foundation – table layouts   67
Time for action – Creating the Categories table   68
Time for action – Defining a script to create the Products table   71
Table columns   72
    Data types of table columns   72
Relations, constraints, and indices   73
    Relations   74
    Constraints   76
Time for action – Adding a constraint to the Product table   77
Time for action – Creating a script to add a check constraint   78
    Indices   79
Time for action – Adding an index using the designer   80
Time for action – Creating a script to add an index   82
Normal form   83
Putting it all together   83
Time for action – Creating a schema for the order entry system   83
Do not use database-generated IDs   89
Views   90

What about stored procedures and triggers	**90**
Summary	**91**
Chapter 5: Mapping the Model to the Database	**93**
What is mapping?	**93**
Types of mapping	**94**
XML-based mapping	94
Attribute-based mapping	97
Fluent mapping	99
Mapping by convention	102
A word about lazy loading	**103**
Loading data on demand	103
Proxies	103
Virtual properties and methods	104
Creating database schema creation scripts	**104**
Fluent mapping	**105**
Expression trees – please explain	106
Getting started	106
Classes	107
Entity level settings	107
ID columns	108
Properties	109
References	111
Collections	111
Mapping many-to-many relations	113
Mapping value objects	113
Time for action – Mapping our domain	**114**
Use mapping conventions	**121**
ID conventions	121
Property conventions	122
Foreign key conventions	123
No mapping; is that possible?	**124**
Auto-mapping with Fluent NHibernate	124
Time for action – Using auto-mapping	**125**
Using ConfORM	129
Time for action – Using ConfORM to map our domain	**129**
XML mapping	**132**
Getting started	133
Classes	134
Properties	134
ID columns	135

Table of Contents

One-to-many relations	136
Many-to-many relations	138
Mapping value objects	139
Time for action – Mapping a simple domain using XML	**139**
Summary	**143**
Chapter 6: Sessions and Transactions	**145**
What are sessions and transactions	145
Session	145
Transaction	146
The session factory	**147**
Creating your first session	**148**
Why do we call Commit?	148
Adding new data to the database	149
Reading data from the database	149
Get versus Load	150
Updating existing data	151
Deleting data	152
First level cache or identity map	**152**
Clearing the cache	154
Refreshing entities in the cache	154
No database operation without a transaction	**154**
Should I use transactions when querying data?	155
NHibernate session versus database session	**155**
Time for action – Creating a session and doing some CRUD	**156**
Session management	**166**
Web-based applications	166
Time for action –Implementing session management for a web application	**167**
WinForm or WPF applications	174
Windows services	174
Unit of Work	**175**
Handling exception	**175**
Second level cache	**176**
Cache regions	177
Second level cache implementations	177
Time for action – Using a second level cache	**178**
Summary	**182**
Chapter 7: Testing, Profiling, Monitoring, and Logging	**183**
Why do we need tests?	**183**
What should we test?	**184**
What about the database?	**184**

Download SQLite	185
Preparing our environment for testing	**186**
Testing the mapping	189
Testing the mapping with Fluent NHibernate	191
Time for action – Creating the base for testing	**191**
Time for action – Using SQLite in our tests	**196**
Testing queries	198
Logging	**202**
Why do we need to log?	202
Logging with Log4Net	203
Time for action – Adding logging to our application	**203**
Setting up logging for NHibernate	206
Time for action – Enable logging in NHibernate	**207**
Monitoring and profiling	**209**
Analyzing log files	209
Using SQL Server Profiler	210
Monitoring and profiling with NHibernate Profiler	210
Time for action – Adding NHibernate Profiler support	**211**
Summary	**215**
Chapter 8: Configuration	**217**
Why do we need a configuration?	**217**
Elements of the configuration	**218**
Which database do we want to use?	218
What byte code provider and proxy factory?	220
Where are our mappings?	221
Do we use second level caching?	221
Do we want to extend NHibernate?	221
XML configuration	**221**
Time for action – Configuring NHibernate using XML	**222**
Configuring NHibernate in code	**227**
Time for action – Configuring NHibernate in code	**227**
Fluent configuration	**233**
Configuring NHibernate with Loquacious	233
Time for action – Using Loquacious to configure NHibernate	**233**
Configuring NHibernate with Fluent NHibernate	242
Convention over configuration	**243**
Summary	**243**
Chapter 9: Writing Queries	**245**
How can we get to our data?	**246**
The LINQ to NHibernate provider	**247**

Defining the root of our query	247
Limiting the number of records returned	248
Filtering a set of records	248
Mapping a set of records	249
Sorting the resulting set	249
Grouping records	250
Forcing a LINQ query to execute immediately	250
Changing from querying the database to querying in-memory objects	251
Creating a report using LINQ to NHibernate	**252**
Time for action – Preparing the system	**252**
Time for action – Creating the reports	**257**
Criteria queries	**260**
Untyped criteria queries	260
Strongly-typed criteria queries	263
Time for action – Using QueryOver to retrieve data	**265**
Hibernate Query Language	**272**
Lazy loading properties	**275**
Executing multiple queries in a batch	**277**
Eager loading versus lazy loading	**279**
Bulk data changes	**282**
Summary	**283**
Chapter 10: Validating the Data to Persist	**285**
What is validation and why is it so important?	**285**
Who owns the database?	**285**
Why, what, and where do we validate?	**287**
Why validate?	287
What data?	287
Where to validate?	288
Validating single properties	**288**
Configuring the validator	289
Defining validation rules	290
Fluently configure validation rules	291
Enforcing validation	291
Time for action – Using property validation	**292**
Validating complex business rules	**297**
Enforcing always valid entities	298
Using validation classes	299
Time for action – Validating user input	**300**
What to do if we don't own the database?	**311**
Summary	**312**

Chapter 11: Common Pitfalls—Things to Avoid — 313
- Requesting the obvious — 314
- Wrong mapping for read-only access — 315
- Blindly relying on NHibernate — 317
- Using implicit transactions — 317
- Using database-generated IDs — 318
- Using LINQ to NHibernate the wrong way — 319
- The trouble with lazy loading — 321
  - The select (n+1) problem — 321
  - Accessing lazy loaded parts after the session is closed — 324
  - Did I just load the whole database? — 325
- Using one model for read and write operations — 325
  - CQRS — 326
- Phantom updates — 328
- Time for action – Causing a phantom update — 328
- Using NHibernate to persist any type of data — 332
- Summary — 333

Appendix: Pop Quiz Answers — 335
- Chapter 2 — 335
  - A First Complete Sample — 335
- Chapter 3 — 335
  - Creating a Model — 335
- Chapter 4 — 335
  - Defining the Database Schema — 335
- Chapter 5 — 336
  - Mapping the Model to the Database — 336
- Chapter 6 — 336
  - Sessions and Transactions — 336
- Chapter 7 — 336
  - Testing, Profiling, Monitoring, and Logging — 336
- Chapter 8 — 336
  - Configuration — 336
- Chapter 9 — 337
  - Writing Queries — 337
- Chapter 10 — 337
  - Validating the Data to Persist — 337

Index — 339

Preface

NHibernate 3 Beginner's Guide examines all of the topics required to get a functional data-access layer implemented while writing the least amount of code possible, presenting options along the way to handle particular edge cases or situations as they arise. The book begins with an introduction to NHibernate 3 and then moves on to creating the development environment. It teaches you how to create a model, define a database schema, and map the model to the database, and then covers sessions and transactions. This is succeeded by testing, profiling and configuration, validation of data, and writing queries. Finally, we wrap up with notes on the common pitfalls that you should avoid.

What this book covers

Chapter 1, *First Look* This chapter explains what NHibernate is and why we would use it in an application that needs to access data in a relational database. The chapter also briefly presents what is the new additions in NHibernate 3.x compared to the versionto version 2.x, and discusses how one can get this framework. It also links to various sources providing documentation and help are presented.

Chapter 2, *A First Complete Sample*. This chapter walks us through a simple yet complete sample, where the core concepts of NHibernate and its usage are introduced.

Chapter 3, *Creating a Model*. This chapter discusses what a domain model is and what building blocks constitute such a model. In an exercise, the reader creates a domain model for a simple ordering system.

Chapter 4, *Defining the Database Schema*. This chapter explains what a database schema is, and describes in details the individual parts comprising such a schema. A schema for the ordering system is created in an exercise.

Preface

Chapter 5, Mapping the Model to the Database. This chapter teaches you how to bridge the gap between the domain model and the database schema, with the aid of some wiring. This chapter, and presents four distinct techniques on how the model can be mapped to the underlying database, or vice versa. It is also shows how we can use NHibernate to automatically create the database schema by leveraging the meta-information contained in the domain model.

Chapter 6, Sessions and Transactions. This chapter teaches you how to create NHibernate sessions to communicate with the database, and how to use transactions to group multiple tasks into one consistent operation which succeeds or fails as a whole.

Chapter 7, Testing, Profiling, Monitoring, and Logging. This chapter introduces how to test and profile our system during development to make sure we deliver a reliable, robust, and maintainable application. It also shows you how an application can be monitored in a productive environment and how it can log any unexpected or faulty behavior.

Chapter 8, Configuration. This chapter explains how we can instruct NHibernate about which database to use, as well as provide it with the necessary credentials to get access to the stored data. Additionally, many more settings for NHibernate are presented that can be to tweaked and will optimize the database access. are explained in this chapter.

Chapter 9, Writing Queries. This chapter discusses the various means on how we can easily and efficiently query data from the database to create meaningful reports on screen or on paper.

Chapter 10, Validating the data to persist. This chapter discusses why data collected by an application needs to be correct, complete, and consistent. It shows how we can instrument NHibernate to achieve this goal through various validation techniques.

Chapter 11, Common Pitfalls – Things to avoid. This chapter, as the last chapter of this book, presents the most common errors developers can make when using NHibernate to write or read data to and from the database. Each such pitfall is discussed in details and possible solutions to overcome the problems are given.

What you need for this book

To successfully complete the examples in this book, you will need a copy of either Visual Studio 2008 or 2010. You can use any version as long as it includes the web application projects. This could be either a Visual Web Developer Express version or any full version such as Professional.

In addition to Visual Studio, you will also need a SQL database server. The examples are generated using SQL Server Express 2008 and SQL Server Management Studio (SSMS) Express.

You will also need to download the NHibernate, Fluent NHibernate, SQLite, and NUnit binary files from sources presented in Chapter 2.

Absolutely no knowledge of NHibernate is required to read this book.

Who this book is for

If you are a new or seasoned developer of .NET web or desktop applications who is looking for a better way to access database data, then this book is for you. It is a basic introduction to NHibernate, with enough information to get a solid foundation in using NHibernate. Some advanced concepts are presented, where appropriate, to enhance functionality, or in situations where they are commonly used.

Conventions

In this book, you will find several headings appearing frequently.

To give clear instructions of how to complete a procedure or task, we use:

Time for action – heading

1. Action 1
2. Action 2
3. Action 3

Instructions often need some extra explanation so that they make sense, so they are followed with:

What just happened?

This heading explains the working of tasks or instructions that you have just completed.

You will also find some other learning aids in the book, including:

Pop quiz – heading

These are short multiple choice questions intended to help you test your own understanding.

Have a go hero – heading

These set practical challenges and give you ideas for experimenting with what you have learned.

You will also find a number of styles of text that distinguish between different kinds of information. Here are some examples of these styles, and an explanation of their meaning.

Code words in text are shown as follows: "We can include other contexts through the use of the `include` directive."

A block of code is set as follows:

```
public class ProductMap : ClassMap<Product>
{
  public ProductMap()
  {
    Id(x =>x.Id);
    Map(x =>x.Name).Length(50).Not.Nullable();
    Map(x =>x.UnitPrice).Not.Nullable();
    Map(x =>x.ReorderLevel).Not.Nullable();
    Map(x =>x.Discontinued).Not.Nullable();
  }
}
```

New terms and **important words** are shown in bold. Words that you see on the screen, in menus or dialog boxes for example, appear in the text like this: "Run the application and click on the **CreateProduct** button".

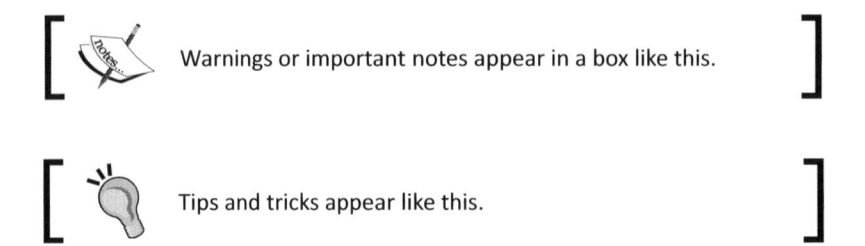

Warnings or important notes appear in a box like this.

Tips and tricks appear like this.

Reader feedback

Feedback from our readers is always welcome. Let us know what you think about this book—what you liked or may have disliked. Reader feedback is important for us to develop titles that you really get the most out of.

To send us general feedback, simply send an e-mail to `feedback@packtpub.com`, and mention the book title via the subject of your message.

If there is a book that you need and would like to see us publish, please send us a note in the **SUGGEST A TITLE** form on `www.packtpub.com` or e-mail `suggest@packtpub.com`.

If there is a topic that you have expertise in and you are interested in either writing or contributing to a book, see our author guide on `www.packtpub.com/authors`.

Customer support

Now that you are the proud owner of a Packt book, we have a number of things to help you to get the most from your purchase.

Downloading the example code

You can download the example code files for all Packt books you have purchased from your account at `http://www.PacktPub.com`. If you purchased this book elsewhere, you can visit `http://www.PacktPub.com/support` and register to have the files e-mailed directly to you.

Errata

Although we have taken every care to ensure the accuracy of our content, mistakes do happen. If you find a mistake in one of our books—maybe a mistake in the text or the code—we would be grateful if you would report this to us. By doing so, you can save other readers from frustration and help us improve subsequent versions of this book. If you find any errata, please report them by visiting `http://www.packtpub.com/support`, selecting your book, clicking on the **errata submission form** link, and entering the details of your errata. Once your errata are verified, your submission will be accepted and the errata will be uploaded on our website, or added to any list of existing errata, under the Errata section of that title. Any existing errata can be viewed by selecting your title from `http://www.packtpub.com/support`.

Piracy

Piracy of copyright material on the Internet is an ongoing problem across all media. At Packt, we take the protection of our copyright and licenses very seriously. If you come across any illegal copies of our works, in any form, on the Internet, please provide us with the location address or website name immediately so that we can pursue a remedy.

Please contact us at `copyright@packtpub.com` with a link to the suspected pirated material.

We appreciate your help in protecting our authors, and our ability to bring you valuable content.

Questions

You can contact us at `questions@packtpub.com` if you are having a problem with any aspect of the book, and we will do our best to address it.

1
First Look

It seems like every single project we begin as developers, no matter how simple, requires some sort of storage. Sometimes, this is a simple collection of values in an XML file or a key-value pair in a properties file.

However, more often than not, we need to have access to larger volumes of data represented in multiple related database tables. In either case, we are generally forced to reinvent the wheel; to create new data retrieval and storage methods for each piece of data that we want to access. Enter NHibernate.

In this chapter, we will discuss:

- What is NHibernate
- What is new in the latest version of NHibernate
- Why we should use it and who else is using it
- Where can we get help or even commercial support when we get lost

What is NHibernate

Put simply, NHibernate is a framework that allows us to talk to a relational database in an object-oriented way. We can store (or as we also often say, "persist") objects in a database and load those objects from the database later on. NHibernate "auto-magically" translates our object-based language to a language that the database understands. That is, NHibernate generates the necessary SQL statements for us to insert, update, delete, and load data.

First Look

If we use NHibernate, then we never have to write any code that deals with the fact that there is an **impedance mismatch** between the way we develop applications in .NET and how a database works. NHibernate has abstracted away this mismatch for us.

Now, let me try to explain what we understand when talking about an impedance mismatch. An application written in .NET is object-oriented. We deal with objects that contain data and logic. Most often, we deal with a single object that communicates with other objects through messages or events. On the other hand, a relational database is all about (big) sets of data. Relational databases are great when it comes to manipulating those sets of data. However, in a relational database, the concept of objects makes no sense. Logic and data live apart.

In a more formal fashion, we can say that NHibernate is an Object Relational Mapper (ORM) tool or framework. NHibernate is a .NET port of Java's Hibernate. It is designed to bring the interactions with the RDBMS solutions in an application code inline with the current object-oriented application design.

NHibernate is not the sole ORM framework for .NET, but it is probably the most mature and feature rich of all. Some of the other frameworks that exist are: Entity Framework from Microsoft, LLBLGen Pro, Subsonic, and Genome, to name just a few. The following screenshot is the NHibernate logo:

What is new in NHibernate 3.0

NHibernate 3.0 introduces a lot of new features as compared to the previous version. The most important ones are as follows:

- NHibernate is now based on .NET 3.5. It makes heavy use of the new concepts that were introduced with this version of the framework. Most notably, this is the usage of expression trees and extension methods. A good sample is the new in-code configuration of NHibernate using a fluent API. As a consequence, NHibernate 3.0 only runs on .NET 3.5 or higher.

- NHibernate now contains in its core a totally rewritten LINQ provider, which supports a large part of the full spectrum of LINQ, and overcomes many of the limitations of the previous LINQ provider. The previous LINQ provider was part of the NHibernate contributions and was based on the criteria API. It only supported a limited set of LINQ queries.

- There is a new QueryOver API available, which combines the use of Extension Methods and Lambda Expressions to provide a statically type-safe wrapper around the ICriteria API.
- A new method has been added about how we can define the mapping between our model and the database. We can now define the mappings in code and add them to the NHibernate configuration. One contribution project already leverages this new possibility. It is called ConfORM. With this API, we can define rules and exceptions to instruct NHibernate how to create our mappings. The whole mapping process is fully convention based. ConfORM is highly extensible and we can easily define our own rules and exceptions.
- It is now possible to lazy load specific columns of a table. This makes sense in scenarios where a table contains BLOB or CLOB fields, which need to be loaded rarely as a result of an explicit request. Previously, only whole objects could be lazy loaded.
- Detached criteria now also work with stateless sessions.

Besides these new features, there have been a lot of bug fixes and stability improvements.

Why would I use it

In the past, we carefully hand-crafted our data access layers for the applications we wrote. We spent as much as 50% or more of our overall time to implement and maintain this data layer. It was not a very challenging task though, and a lot of repetitive coding was involved. For each and every single type of object we wanted to persist in the database, we had to write similar code. We had to write code to insert a new object into the database, to update an existing object in the database, and to delete an existing object from the database. Furthermore, we wrote code to read an existing single object or a list of existing objects from the database. At a minimum, we had to write six methods per object type.

Somehow, we realized that writing this data layer did not really add value to our business application. It didn't make our application specific as it was only infrastructure code. For each and every application we wrote, we had to implement similar code; be it an ordering system used in an e-commerce or a facility management system for an airport, or a portfolio management, or a trading system for a bank. All types of applications needed the same kind of data access layer.

As we were so bored by always writing the same kind of code again and again, we started to think about the possibility to automate this process as much as possible. The first approach was to write code generators, which, based on certain configuration and templates, wrote the data access code for us. This worked to a certain extent. We were very happy about it, as now, finally, we had more time to concentrate on the important problems such as writing and maintaining the business logic and the user interface, which made our applications unique and added real business value to the overall solution.

As we were not the only developers facing the problem of writing the data access code, some people started to write and publish a framework that would solve this problem. This was the birth of the ORM frameworks such as NHibernate.

Nowadays, accessing relational data from an object-oriented application is a solved problem, period! Why would you want to reinvent the wheel? There is absolutely nothing left that is new or yet unresolved. Data access code is not specific to a certain problem domain. (This statement is even true in regard of new storage technologies such as document databases, Google's big table, and others.)

Every application that needs to manipulate data reads and writes this data from or to the data store in exactly the same way.

Thus, writing your own data layer is a waste of time. Somebody even used a much more pronounced phrase to pinpoint this fact, "Writing your own data access layer is like stealing money from your client".

Where do I get it

The home of the NHibernate project is at `http://www.nhforge.org`, while the code is housed at SourceForge (`http://sourceforge.net/projects/nhibernate/`). NHibernate is an open source project (OSS). Thus, the code and/or the binaries are freely available and can be downloaded from SourceForge.

Throughout this book, we also make use of Fluent NHibernate, which is a sister project of NHibernate and provides a way to fluently define the NHibernate mappings between the model and database. It is also an OSS project and binaries and/or source code can be downloaded from `http://fluentnhibernate.org/downloads`.

In a later chapter, we will also use a NHibernate contribution project for the validation of the domain entities. The set of NHibernate contribution projects can be downloaded from `http://sourceforge.net/projects/nhcontrib/`.

If you use Visual Studio 2010 Professional or higher, then there is an even easier method available as to how we can get to the necessary NHibernate (or Fluent NHibernate) binaries. We can use the **NuGet** extension for Visual Studio to download NHibernate and all its dependencies and automatically make those binaries a part of our projects. The NuGet project (`http://nuget.codeplex.com/`) is a free, open source package management system for .NET. It is led and sponsored by Microsoft. At the time of writing, the NuGet project is at version 1.3 and is still under heavy development. Nevertheless, it feels ready for professional use and can really simplify the way we add external dependencies, such as NHibernate or Fluent NHibernate, to our solutions. The following screenshot is the NuGet logo:

Is there documentation available

Unlike with a commercial product, there is no manual available for NHibernate. However, there is a website that is fully dedicated to NHibernate. This website can be found at `http://www.nhforge.org` and contains a lot of useful information about and around NHibernate. There is also a reference document published on this website. The reference documentation is very detailed and complete, and should be one of the first sources to consult whenever dealing with a very specific problem or setting. There are also many beginners guides, tutorials, and blog posts that can be found here.

The following list presents a couple of blogs that are either mostly dedicated to NHibernate or contain a lot of information around this framework:

- NHibernate meta blog at `http://nhforge.org/blogs/nhibernate`.
- NHibernate FAQs at `http://nhibernate.hibernatingrhinos.com/`.
- Fabio Maulo's blog at `http://fabiomaulo.blogspot.com`. Fabio is the leader of the NHibernate project.
- Ayende Rahien's blog at `http://ayende.com/Blog/default.aspx`. Ayende is one of the main contributors to NHibernate. Search for NHibernate.
- James Gregory's blog at `http://jagregory.com`. James is the leader of the Fluent NHibernate project.

Quite a few books have been written about NHibernate so far. The latest one being the *NHibernate 3.0 Cookbook*, which is written for intermediate to advanced users of NHibernate. The detailed list of books is as follows:

- "Hibernate in Action" by Christian Bauer and Gavin King, Manning Publications Co.: This is probably the first book published about Hibernate and discusses the Java version of the framework
- "NHibernate in Action" by Pierre Henri Kuaté, Tobin Harris, Christian Bauer, Gavin King, and Tobin Harris Manning Publications Co.
- "NHibernate 2 Beginner's Guide" by Aaron Cure, Packt Publishing
- "NHibernate 3.0 Cookbook" by Jason Dentler, Packt Publishing

Can I get help using NHibernate

For any questions you might have regarding NHibernate, there is a Google Group called "NHibernate Users Mailing List". This mailing list is very active and questions are usually answered within hours, if not within minutes. The list can be found at http://groups.google.com/group/nhusers. At the time of writing, this list contained nearly 30,000 messages. The list can be searched by any keyword and is a good source of tips and hints about how to use NHibernate in various very specific circumstances. Mostly, we can find a solution to our problem in one of the existing message threads without even having to post our own question first. This is shown in the following screenshot:

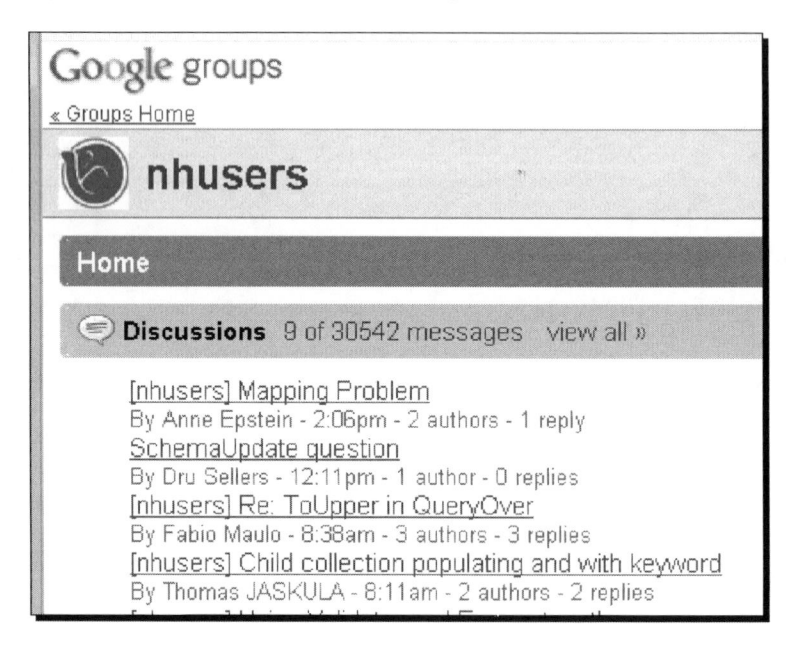

In addition to this (English) group, there exist several language specific (sub-) groups. Currently, there exist groups in Spanish, French, Italian, Portuguese, German, Dutch, and Chinese. The complete list of groups can be found at `http://nhforge.org/groups`.

One of the more active groups is the Chinese group. The Chinese community not only has a forum, but also a community site at `http://home.cnblogs.com/groups/NHibernate`. They are currently working on a new community site at `http://nhplex.com/`.

If you want to discuss the development of NHibernate or become a contributor to the project, then there is also a mailing list available for this purpose: `http://groups.google.com/group/nhibernate-development`.

Is there commercial support available

NHibernate has a rich and vibrant community, and there are many community-based support channels which are absolutely free, as mentioned in the previous section.

However, there are situations where you really want to have someone you can call to get immediate help. Or maybe your company doesn't want to use a technology without having a signed support contract at hand.

At the time of writing, commercial support for NHibernate is available at least from `http://nhprof.com/CommercialSupport`.

Who uses it

NHibernate is a mature and stable framework and has been around for many years. Many companies have been using it in many different projects. A lot of those projects are mission critical to the respective companies. Other applications that use NHibernate are exposed to high load and perform very well under these stressful circumstances.

Due to political reasons, not all companies wish to disclose their usage of NHibernate.

However, there is still a list of success stories available on the NHibernate website. This list can be found by using the following link:

`http://nhforge.org/wikis/successstories/success-stories.aspx`

Summary

In this chapter, we have learned what NHibernate is and why we would want to use it. We also briefly discussed the new important features that NHibernate 3.0 brings to the table. As an important aspect, we got all the information we need to find abundant documentation about NHibernate and get community-driven help or even commercial support (if needed). We also learned that NHibernate has a very broad user base and is driving many critical projects around the world in companies of all sectors.

To give you some numbers: over 100 thousand downloads have been registered so far for NHibernate 2.1.2, and more than 35 thousand downloads for NHibernate 3.0 in its first three months of availability.

2
A First Complete Sample

So far you have learned what NHibernate is and why it makes sense to use it when developing a new application. Now it is time to show how easy it is to use NHibernate in a real world application. We will create, with minimal effort, a fully working sample that allows us to write to and subsequently, read data from a database.

In this chapter, we shall:

- Prepare our system to enable development of applications using NHibernate
- Create a simple model of a problem domain
- Create a database and define a mapping between the model and the database
- Write and read data to and from the database
- Discuss what we would have to do to achieve the same goal without NHibernate or any other ORM tool

So let's get on with it.

Prepare our development environment

In this book, I am assuming that you have a computer at hand which has Windows Vista, Windows 7, Windows Server 2003 or Windows Server 2008 installed. If you are using an Apple computer, then you can install, for example, Windows 7 as a virtual machine.

First, install Microsoft Visual Studio 2010 Professional, Microsoft Visual C# 2010 Express or Microsoft Visual Basic 2010 Express on your system. The Express editions of Visual Studio can be downloaded from http://www.microsoft.com/express/windows.

> Note that NHibernate 3.x can also be used with the 2008 editions of Microsoft Visual Studio, but not with any older versions. NHibernate 3.x is based on the .NET framework version 3.5, and thus only works with IDEs that support this or a higher version of the .NET framework.

Additionally, note that if you don't want to use Visual Studio, then there are at least two other free OSS options available to you:

- MonoDevelop is an IDE primarily designed for C# and other .NET languages. MonoDevelop makes it easy for developers to port .NET applications created with Visual Studio to Linux and to maintain a single code base for all platforms. MonoDevelop 2.4 or higher can be downloaded from `http://monodevelop.com/download`.

- SharpDevelop is a free IDE for C#, VB.NET, and Boo projects on Microsoft's .NET platform. It is open source. SharpDevelop 3.2 or higher can be downloaded from `http://sharpdevelop.net/OpenSource/SD/Default.aspx`.

Furthermore, note that NHibernate also works on Mono: `http://www.mono-project.com`.

Next, we need a relational database to play with. NHibernate supports all major relational databases like Oracle, MS SQL Server, MySQL, and so on. In this book, we will use MS SQL Server as our Relational Database Management System (RDBMS). We will also use SQLite in Chapter 7 when writing tests.

> To use SQL Server as the database server throughout this book is not a casual choice. Microsoft SQL Server is the most used RDBMS in conjunction with NHibernate and, in general, with .NET projects.
>
> The SQL Server driver for NHibernate is one of the most tested drivers in NHibernate's suite of unit tests, and when specific new features come out, it is likely that they will be first supported by this driver.

Install the free Microsoft SQL Server 2008 R2 Express on your system if you have not already done so during the install of Visual Studio. You can download the express edition of MS SQL Server from here `http://www.microsoft.com/express/Database/`. For our samples, it really doesn't matter which version you download: the 32-bit or the 64-bit version. Just take the one that matches best with the bitness of your operating system. Make sure that you install SQL Server with the default instance name of SQL Express. If this is not possible for you, then you will need to adjust the connection string settings in the samples we develop throughout this book.

Make sure you also download and install the free SQL Server Management Studio Express (SSMS) from the following link:

`http://www.microsoft.com/download/en/details.aspx?id=22985`.

Now, we are ready to tackle NHibernate. We can download NHibernate 3.1.0 GA from Source Forge `http://sourceforge.net/projects/nhibernate/`. The download consists of a single ZIP file containing the following content, as shown in the screenshot:

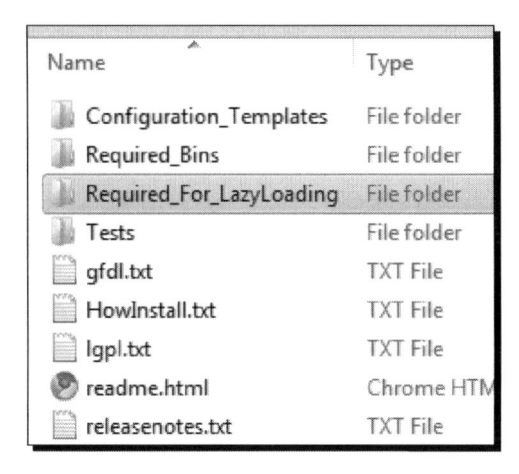

Name	Type
Configuration_Templates	File folder
Required_Bins	File folder
Required_For_LazyLoading	File folder
Tests	File folder
gfdl.txt	TXT File
HowInstall.txt	TXT File
lgpl.txt	TXT File
readme.html	Chrome HTM
releasenotes.txt	TXT File

The binaries that are always needed when developing an NHibernate based application can be found in the `Required_Bins` folder. Opening this folder, we find the files as shown in the following screenshot:

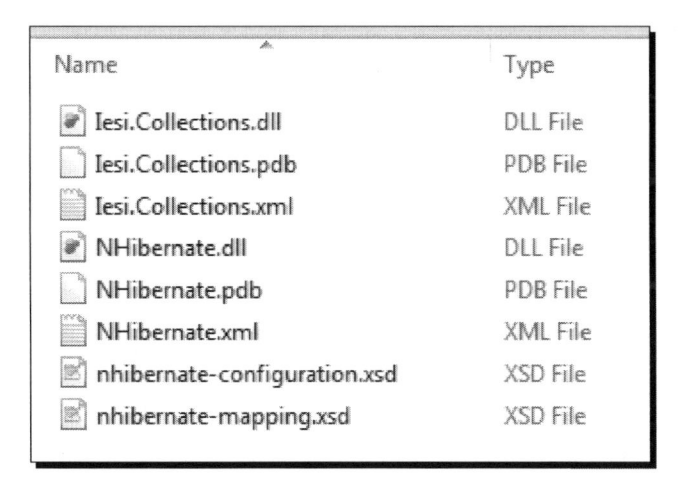

Name	Type
Iesi.Collections.dll	DLL File
Iesi.Collections.pdb	PDB File
Iesi.Collections.xml	XML File
NHibernate.dll	DLL File
NHibernate.pdb	PDB File
NHibernate.xml	XML File
nhibernate-configuration.xsd	XSD File
nhibernate-mapping.xsd	XSD File

> Note that if you are downloading version 3.1 or newer of NHibernate, you will no longer find the two DLLs, `Antlr3.Runtime.dll` and `Remotion.Data.Linq.dll`, in the ZIP file that were present in version 3.0. The reason is that they have been IL merged into the `NHibernate.dll`.

If we want to use lazy loading with NHibernate (and we surely will), then we also have to use some additional files which can be found in the `Required_For_LazyLoading` folder.

> Lazy loading is a technique that is used to load certain parts of the data only when really needed, which is when the code accesses it. Lazy loading will be discussed in detail in subsequent chapters of this book.

There are three different options at hand. We want to choose Castle. The corresponding folder contains these files, as shown in the following screenshot:

Name	Type
Castle.Core.dll	DLL File
Castle.Core.xml	XML File
NHibernate.ByteCode.Castle.dll	DLL File
NHibernate.ByteCode.Castle.pdb	PDB File
NHibernate.ByteCode.Castle.xml	XML File

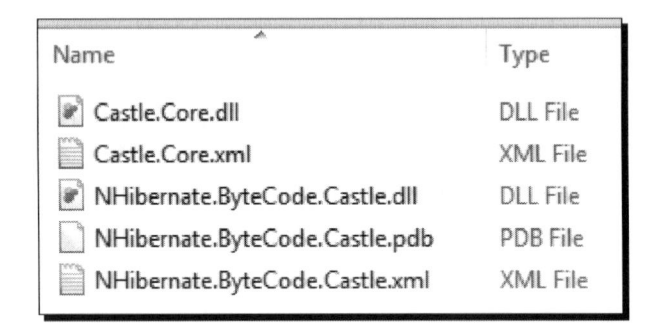

As we are also using Fluent NHibernate throughout the samples in this book, we want to download the corresponding binaries too. Go grab the binaries from the Fluent NHibernate website and copy them to the appropriate location on your system. In either case, there is no installer available or needed. We just have to copy a bunch of files to a folder we define. Please download Fluent NHibernate, which also contains the binaries for NHibernate, from here (`http://fluentnhibernate.org/downloads`), as shown in the following screenshot. Make sure you download the binaries for NHibernate 3.1 and not an earlier version.

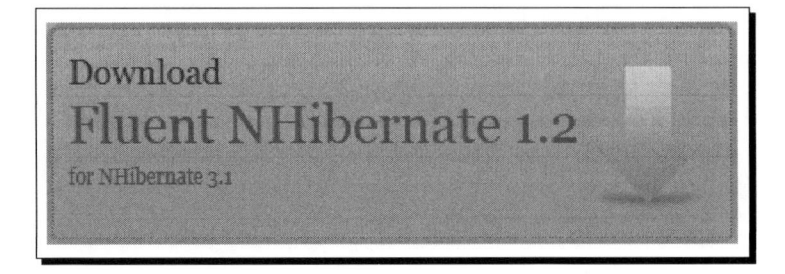

Download
Fluent NHibernate 1.2
for NHibernate 3.1

Save the ZIP file you just downloaded to a location where you can easily find it for later usage. The ZIP file contains the files shown in the following screenshot:

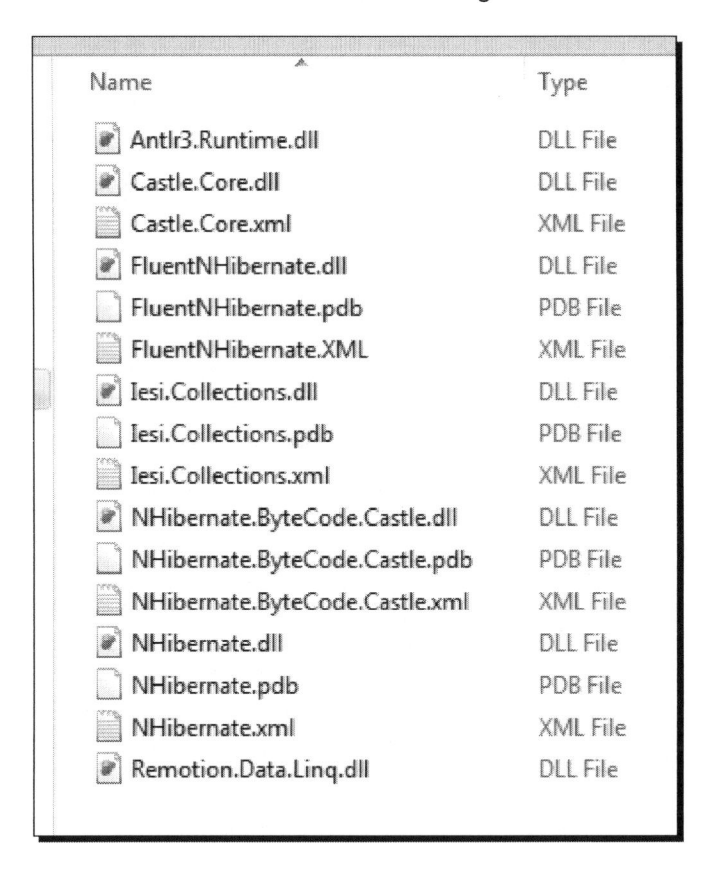

Name	Type
Antlr3.Runtime.dll	DLL File
Castle.Core.dll	DLL File
Castle.Core.xml	XML File
FluentNHibernate.dll	DLL File
FluentNHibernate.pdb	PDB File
FluentNHibernate.XML	XML File
Iesi.Collections.dll	DLL File
Iesi.Collections.pdb	PDB File
Iesi.Collections.xml	XML File
NHibernate.ByteCode.Castle.dll	DLL File
NHibernate.ByteCode.Castle.pdb	PDB File
NHibernate.ByteCode.Castle.xml	XML File
NHibernate.dll	DLL File
NHibernate.pdb	PDB File
NHibernate.xml	XML File
Remotion.Data.Linq.dll	DLL File

The only additional files regarding the direct NHibernate download are the `FluentNHibernate.*` files. On the other hand, we do not have the XSD schema files (`nhibernate-configuration.xsd` and `nhibernate-mapping.xsd`) included in this package and we'll want to copy those from the NHibernate package when implementing our sample.

A First Complete Sample

Defining a model

After we have successfully downloaded the necessary NHibernate and Fluent NHibernate files, we are ready to start implementing our first application using NHibernate. Let's first model the problem domain we want to create the application for. The domain for which we want to build our application is a product inventory system. With the application, we want to be able to manage a list of products for a small grocery store. The products shall be grouped by category. A category consists of a name and a short description. The product on the other hand has a name, a short description, a category, a unit price, a reorder level, and a flag to determine whether it is discontinued or not. To uniquely identify each category and product, they each have an ID. If we draw a class diagram of the model just described, then it would look similar to the following screenshot:

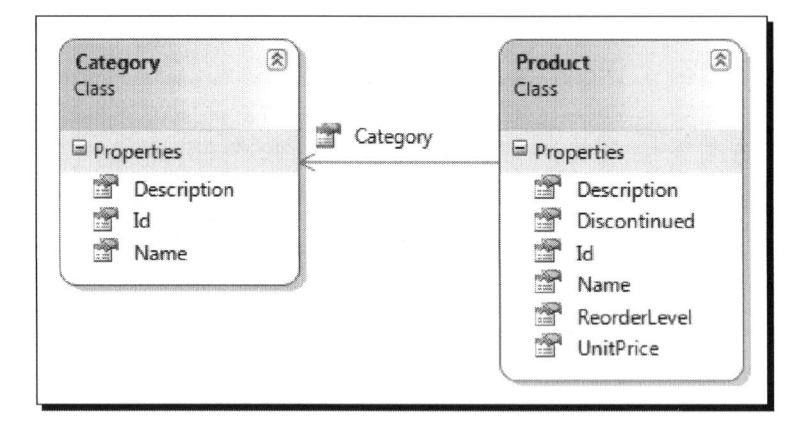

Category — Class
Properties:
- Description
- Id
- Name

Category →

Product — Class
Properties:
- Description
- Discontinued
- Id
- Name
- ReorderLevel
- UnitPrice

Unfortunately, the class designer used to create the preceding screenshot is only available in the professional version of Visual Studio and not in the free Express editions.

Time for action – Creating the product inventory model

Let's implement the model for our simple product inventory system. First, we want to define a location on our system, where we will put all our code that we create for this and the subsequent chapters.

1. Create a folder called `NH3BeginnersGuide` on your file system. Inside this new folder, create another folder called `lib`. This is the place where we will put all the assemblies needed to develop an application using NHibernate and Fluent NHibernate.

2. Locate the ZIP file containing the Fluent NHibernate files that you downloaded in the first section of this chapter. Extract all files to the `lib` folder created in the preceding step.

3. Open Visual Studio and create a new project. Choose **WPF Application** as the project template. Call the project **Chapter2**. Make sure that the solution you create will be saved in the folder `NH3BeginnersGuide` you created in the preceding step. When using VS 2008 Pro, you can do this when creating the new project. If, on the other hand, you use the Express edition of Visual Studio, then you choose the location when you first save your project.

4. Add a new class to the project and call it `Category`. To this class, add a virtual (auto-) property called `Id`, which is of the `int` type. Also, add two other virtual properties of the `string` type, called `Name` and `Description`. The code should look similar to the following code snippet:

```
namespace Chapter2
{
  public class Category
  {
    public virtual int Id { get; set; }
    public virtual string Name { get; set; }
    public virtual string Description { get; set; }
  }
}
```

Downloading the example code

You can download the example code files for all Packt books you have purchased from your account at `http://www.PacktPub.com`. If you purchased this book elsewhere, you can visit `http://www.PacktPub.com/support` and register to have the files e-mailed directly to you.

A First Complete Sample

5. Add another class to the project and call it `Product`. To this class, add the properties, as shown in the following code snippet. The type of the respective property is given in parenthesis:
`Id` (`int`), `Name` (`string`), `Description` (`string`), `Category` (`Category`), `UnitPrice` (`decimal`), `ReorderLevel` (`int`), and `Discontinued` (`bool`). The resulting code should look similar to the following code snippet:

```
namespace Chapter2
{
  public class Product
  {
    public virtual int Id { get; set; }
    public virtual string Name { get; set; }
    public virtual string Description { get; set; }
    public virtual Category Category { get; set; }
    public virtual decimal UnitPrice { get; set; }
    public virtual int ReorderLevel { get; set; }
    public virtual bool Discontinued { get; set; }
  }
}
```

What just happened?

We have implemented the two classes `Category` and `Product`, which define our simple domain model. Each attribute of the entity is implemented as a virtual property of the class. To limit the amount of code necessary to define the entities, we use auto properties. Note that the properties are all declared as virtual. This is needed as NHibernate uses lazy loading by default. The details and implications of lazy loading will be discussed in more detail in subsequent chapters of this book.

Mapping our model

Now that we have defined and implemented the model for our simple product inventory application, we need to instruct NHibernate how to map our model classes to the underlying tables in the database. The mapping is responsible to define which class maps to which table, and which property of a class maps to which column of a table. Having defined this information, NHibernate can successfully operate and create the necessary SQL statements that allow us to add, update, and delete data in the database, as well as query existing data.

Various methods exist to show how we can define the mappings. Probably, the most common methods are either to define the mappings in the form of XML documents or to define them in code. In this chapter, we will choose the latter method.

Time for action – Creating the mapping classes

To make our life very simple, we will use Fluent NHibernate to map our model to the underlying database. Fluent NHibernate allows us to define the mapping in code, in a type-safe way.

1. Add a reference to `FluentNHibernate.dll` and to `NHibernate.dll`, which you can locate in the `lib` folder, as shown in the following screenshot:

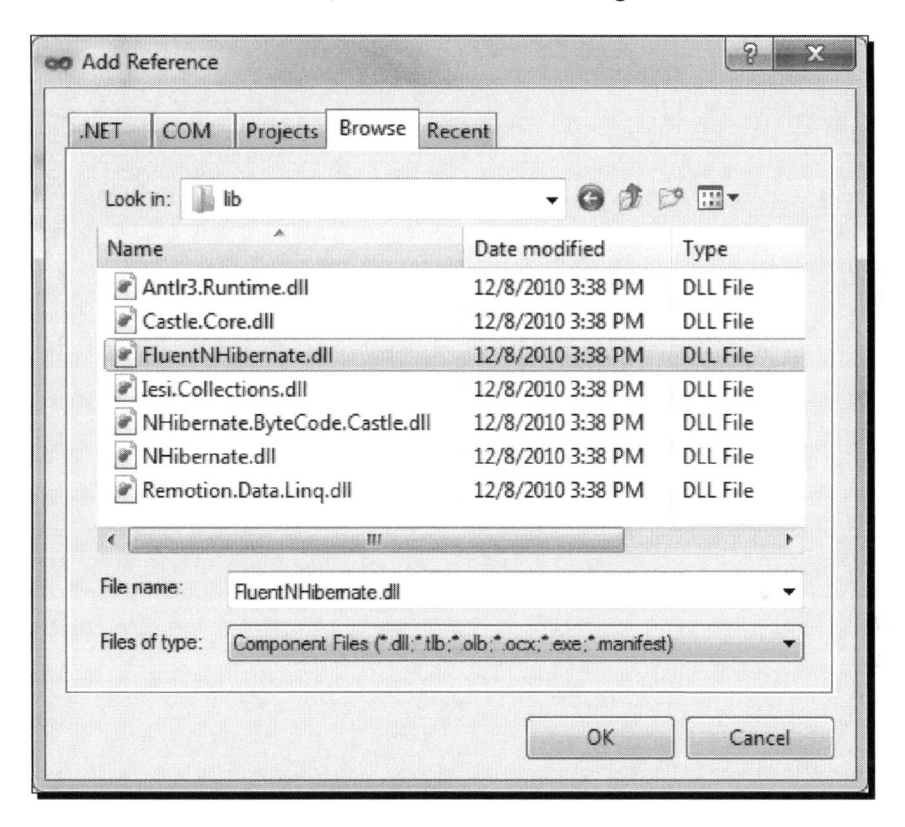

2. Add a new class to the project and call it `CategoryMap`. Add `using FluentNHibernate.Mapping;` to the file.

3. Make the class inherit from `ClassMap<Category>`.

4. Add a default constructor to the class and define the mapping for the `Id`.

A First Complete Sample

5. In the constructor, add `Id(x =>x.Id);`, that is, we use the `Id` method defined in the base class to define the mapping of `Id`. The `Id` method expects a lambda expression which identifies the property of the class `Category`, which shall be mapped as `Id`.

6. Furthermore, in the constructor, add `Map(x =>x.Name);` to define the mapping for the `Name` property.

7. Do the same thing for the `Description` property. The resulting code should look similar to the following code snippet:

```
using FluentNHibernate.Mapping;

namespace Chapter2
{
  public class CategoryMap : ClassMap<Category>
  {
    public CategoryMap()
    {
      Id(x => x.Id);
      Map(x => x.Name);
      Map(x => x.Description);
    }
  }
}
```

8. Add another class called `ProductMap` to the project and add the same `using` statement to the file as in the `CategoryMap` file. Make the class inherit from `ClassMap<Product>` and also add a default constructor.

9. In the default constructor, add code to map the property `Id` as the primary key.

10. Furthermore, add code to map the properties: `Name`, `Description`, `UnitPrice`, `ReorderLevel`, and `Discontinued`.

11. Finally, use `References(x =>x.Category);` to map the `Category` property. When done, your code should look similar to the following code snippet:

```
using FluentNHibernate.Mapping;

namespace Chapter2
{
  public class ProductMap : ClassMap<Product>
  {
    public ProductMap()
    {
```

```
            Id(x => x.Id);
            Map(x => x.Name);
            Map(x => x.Description);
            Map(x => x.UnitPrice);
            Map(x => x.ReorderLevel);
            Map(x => x.Discontinued);
            References(x => x.Category);
        }
    }
}
```

> Make sure all your classes (that is, `Category`, `Product`, `CategoryMap`, and `ProductMap`) are defined as `public`. If these classes are not defined as `public`, NHibernate will not be able to discover and use them.

What just happened?

We have defined two classes which provide NHibernate with detailed information about how the model classes `Category` and `Product` can be mapped to an underlying database containing two compatible tables for each `Category` and `Product` class, respectively. Looking at the code, it seems to be very little information that we provide to NHibernate to do its job, but the nice thing is that Fluent NHibernate uses a lot of predefined and meaningful defaults if not defined otherwise.

Creating the database schema

We have defined a model for our problem domain and have defined the necessary information that NHibernate needs to map the model to an underlying database. Now we need to create this database. However, we do not want to handcraft the database schema, but rather let NHibernate create the database schema for us. The only thing we need to do manually is create a new empty database.

NHibernate will use the meta information we provided via the definition of the mapping classes to create an appropriate database schema.

A First Complete Sample

Time for action – Creating the database

First, we will manually create an empty new database and then we will add code to our application, which allows us to delete and recreate the database schema.

1. Open the Microsoft SQL Server Management Studio (**SSMS**), which was installed as part of the MS SQL Server Express setup. When asked for the connection details, enter **.\SQLExpress** as the server name and choose **Windows Authentication** as the authentication mode. This is shown in the following screenshot:

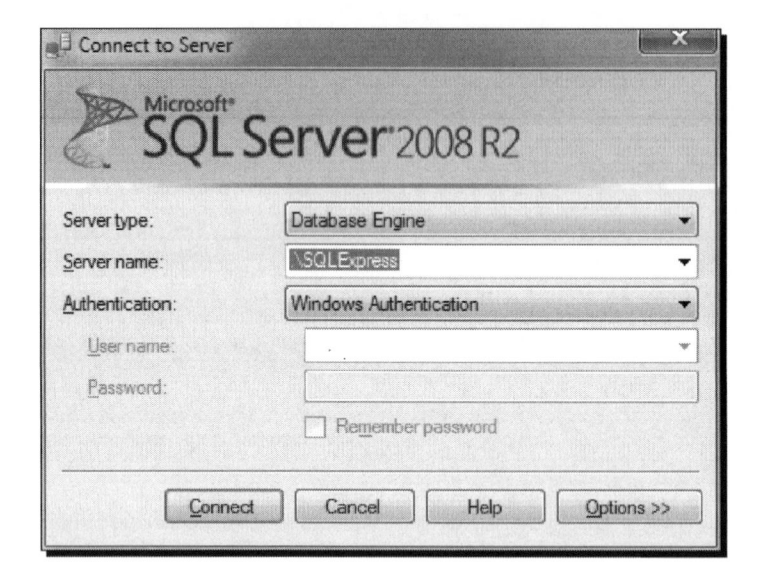

> If you are accessing your locally installed SQL Server Express edition, then you can also use the alias (local) instead of .\SQLExpress to connect to your database.

2. Right-click on the **Databases** folder and select **New Database...**. Enter **NH3BeginnersGuide** as the database name and click on **OK**. A new empty database will be created for you.

3. Back in Visual Studio, open the `MainWindow.xaml` file and modify XAML, as shown in the following code snippet, to create a window with the title **Product Inventory** displaying one button with the text `Create Database`:

```
<Window x:Class="Chapter2.MainWindow"
  xmlns="http://schemas.microsoft.com/winfx/
    2006/xaml/presentation"
  xmlns:x="http://schemas.microsoft.com/winfx/2006/xaml"
  Title="Product Inventory" Height="350" Width="525">
```

```
        <Grid>
          <Grid.RowDefinitions>
            <RowDefinition Height="Auto" />
          </Grid.RowDefinitions>
        <Button x:Name="btnCreateDatabase"
          Content="Create Database"
          Click="btnCreateDatabase_Click"/>
        </Grid>
</Window>
```

4. Open the preceding code file of `MainWindow` (the `MainWindow.xaml.cs` file) and implement the code which defines a connection string to access our **NH3BeginnerGuide** database on SQL Server. This is shown in the following code snippet:

```
const string connString = "server=.\\SQLExpress;" +
    "database=NH3BeginnersGuide;" +
    "Integrated Security=SSPI;";
```

5. Add the following `using` statements at the top of the `MainWindow.xaml.cs` file:

```
using FluentNHibernate.Cfg;
using FluentNHibernate.Cfg.Db;
using NHibernate.Cfg;
using NHibernate.Tool.hbm2ddl;
```

6. Use the `Fluently` class of Fluent NHibernate to define a configuration which will allow us to ask NHibernate to create the database schema via the `CreateSchema` method passed as a parameter to the `ExposeConfiguration` method:

```
Fluently.Configure()
    .Database(MsSqlConfiguration
      .MsSql2008
      .ConnectionString(connString))
    .Mappings(m =>m.FluentMappings.AddFromAssemblyOf<ProductMap>())
    .ExposeConfiguration(CreateSchema)
    .BuildConfiguration();
```

7. In the `CreateSchema` method, use the `SchemaExport` class of NHibernate to delete and create the schema based on the metadata available through the configuration files, as shown in the following code snippet:

```
private static void CreateSchema(Configuration cfg)
{
  var schemaExport = new SchemaExport(cfg);
  schemaExport.Drop(false, true);
  schemaExport.Create(false, true);
}
```

A First Complete Sample

8. Putting all the preceding code together, `MainWindow` should look similar to the following code snippet:

```
using System.Windows;
using FluentNHibernate.Cfg;
using FluentNHibernate.Cfg.Db;
using NHibernate.Cfg;
using NHibernate.Tool.hbm2ddl;

namespace Chapter2
{
  public partial class MainWindow
  {
    const string connString = "server=.\\SQLExpress;" +
      "database=NH3BeginnersGuide;" +
      "Integrated Security=SSPI;";

    public MainWindow()
    {
      InitializeComponent();
    }

    private void btnCreateDatabase_Click(object sender,
      RoutedEventArgs e)
    {
      Fluently.Configure()
        .Database(MsSqlConfiguration
          .MsSql2008
          .ConnectionString(connString))
        .Mappings(m =>m.FluentMappings
          .AddFromAssemblyOf<ProductMap>())
        .ExposeConfiguration(CreateSchema)
        .BuildConfiguration();
    }

    private static void CreateSchema(Configuration cfg)
    {
      var schemaExport = new SchemaExport(cfg);
      schemaExport.Drop(false, true);
      schemaExport.Create(false, true);
    }
  }
}
```

9. Run the application and click on the **Create Database** button. Verify within SSMS that the database **NH3BeginnersGuide** now contains two tables called **Category** and **Product**, respectively. Furthermore, verify that the tables contain a column for each property of the respective class, as shown in the following screenshot:

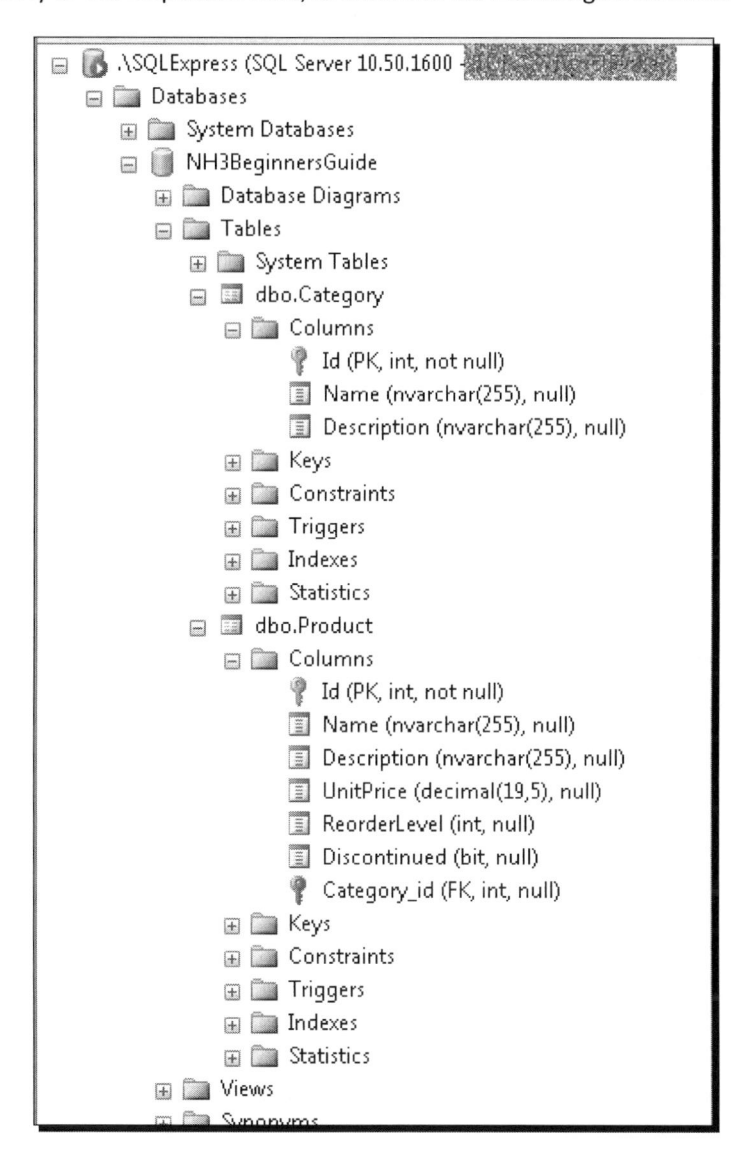

```
─ .\SQLExpress (SQL Server 10.50.1600 -
   ─ Databases
      ⊕ System Databases
      ─ NH3BeginnersGuide
         ⊕ Database Diagrams
         ─ Tables
            ⊕ System Tables
            ─ dbo.Category
               ─ Columns
                  🔑 Id (PK, int, not null)
                  ▤ Name (nvarchar(255), null)
                  ▤ Description (nvarchar(255), null)
               ⊕ Keys
               ⊕ Constraints
               ⊕ Triggers
               ⊕ Indexes
               ⊕ Statistics
            ─ dbo.Product
               ─ Columns
                  🔑 Id (PK, int, not null)
                  ▤ Name (nvarchar(255), null)
                  ▤ Description (nvarchar(255), null)
                  ▤ UnitPrice (decimal(19,5), null)
                  ▤ ReorderLevel (int, null)
                  ▤ Discontinued (bit, null)
                  🔑 Category_id (FK, int, null)
               ⊕ Keys
               ⊕ Constraints
               ⊕ Triggers
               ⊕ Indexes
               ⊕ Statistics
         ⊕ Views
         ⊕ Synonyms
```

A First Complete Sample

What just happened?

We have used SSMS to define an empty new SQL Server database. We then created a new WPF application with a single button on the main window. When we run the application, we can trigger code by clicking on the button which creates an NHibernate configuration object. This object is then used in conjunction with the `SchemaExport` class of NHibernate to create the database schema in the previously defined database.

Creating a session factory

To create sessions through which we can access the database, we need a session factory. Every session object that we ever need has to be created with the aid of such a session factory. Once again, we can use the classes provided by Fluent NHibernate to make things simple. We use the `Fluently` helper class to define, in a fluent way, the necessary information NHibernate needs to be able to create a session factory for us.

Specifically, we have to define what database product and which version of it we are going to use. We also have to define where Fluent NHibernate can find all the mapping files we have written. This leads us to the following code:

```
private ISessionFactory CreateSessionFactory()
{
   return Fluently.Configure()
     .Database(MsSqlConfiguration
       .MsSql2008
       .ConnectionString(connString))
     .Mappings(m =>m.FluentMappings
       .AddFromAssemblyOf<ProductMap>())
     .BuildSessionFactory();
}
```

The preceding method creates a session factory for an MS SQL Server version 2008. It uses the settings of `connString` when connecting to the database. We further instruct Fluent NHibernate to parse the assembly in which `ProductMap` is implemented for any mapping classes. With all this information, we instruct NHibernate to create the factory by calling `BuildSessionFactory()`.

Time for action – Creating a session factory

We now want to write the code necessary to create a session factory for our product inventory application.

1. Add a reference `NHibernate.ByteCode.Castle.dll` to the project. This file can be found in the `lib` folder. NHibernate needs this assembly to create proxies.

2. Add a `using NHibernate` statement to the preceding code of `MainWindow` (the `MainWindow.xaml.cs` file).

3. Add a `CreateSessionFactory` method, as described above, to the preceding code.

4. Extend the grid of `MainWindow` with another row with a height set to `Auto`.

5. Add another button to the `MainWindow` and name it `btnCreateSessionFactory` and define its content as `Create Session Factory`. Set the `Grid.Row` to 1. Furthermore, define a click event handler for this new button. The definition of the `Grid` should look similar to the following code snippet:

   ```xml
   <Grid>
     <Grid.RowDefinitions>
       <RowDefinition Height="Auto" />
       <RowDefinition Height="Auto" />
     </Grid.RowDefinitions>
     <Button x:Name="btnCreateDatabase"
       Content="Create Database"
       Click="btnCreateDatabase_Click"/>
     <Button x:Name="btnCreateSessionFactory"
       Content="Create Session Factory"
       Click="btnCreateSessionFactory_Click"
       Grid.Row="1"/>
   </Grid>
   ```

6. In the click event handler for this new button, enter the following code:

   ```
   var factory = CreateSessionFactory();
   ```

7. Start the application and test whether you can successfully create a session factory, as shown in the following screenshot:

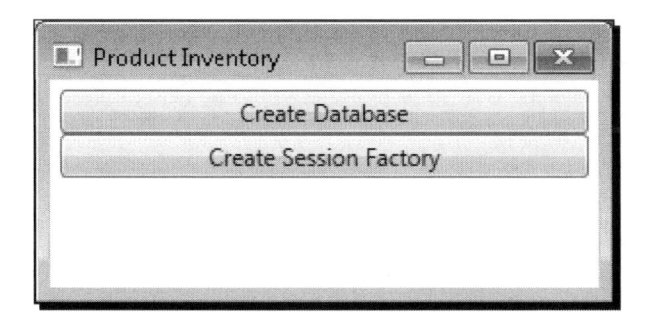

A First Complete Sample

What just happened?

We have added a second button to the main window of our application. In the click event handler of this button, we have implemented the code that creates a new NHibernate session factory. We built the session factory with the aid of the `Fluently` helper class provided by Fluent NHibernate. The session factory can then be used to create session objects used to access the database created in the preceding exercise.

Opening a session

Our application needs a session object to communicate with the database when writing or reading data. As mentioned above, session objects can only be obtained through a session factory. Once we have constructed a session factory, opening a session is a quick and cheap operation. After we have finished using our session object, we must not forget to close the session and dispose it. We can use a `using` statement to instruct the compiler to do this automatically for us.

Time for action – Opening a session to the database

We will implement the code such that our product inventory application can open a session to the database.

1. Add another row to the grid of `MainWindow`. In this new third row, place an additional button called `btnCreateSession` with content `Create Session`. Furthermore, define an event handler for the click event. The code for the button should look similar to the following code snippet:

    ```
    <Button x:Name="btnCreateSession"
      Content="Create Session"
      Click="btnCreateSession_Click"
      Grid.Row="2"/>
    ```

2. In the event handler of this button, add the following code:

    ```
    private void btnCreateSession_Click(object sender,
       RoutedEventArgs e)
    {
      var factory = CreateSessionFactory();
      using (var session = factory.OpenSession())
      {
        // do something with the session
      }
    }
    ```

3. Start the application and verify that you can indeed open a session to the database.

What just happened?

We added yet another button to the main window of the application whose click event handler contains the code to first create a session factory by using the code implemented in the preceding exercise. This session factory is then used to open a session object. We have not yet done anything meaningful with this session object. To use the session will be part of the next exercise.

Persisting objects to the database

The whole ceremony of defining mappings, creating a database schema, creating a session factory, and finally creating and opening a session object has one single purpose: we want to persist the data created by our product inventory application to a durable data store.

Let's first create a new category object. We can do this by using the following code snippet:

```
var category = new Category
  {
    Name = "Beverages",
    Description = "Some description"
  };
```

Next, we want to save this new category object and we can do so by using the following code:

```
var id = session.Save(category);
```

The value that is returned from the save method corresponds to the ID of the newly created category object.

Now, let's create a product. The product has a reference to a category object. Before we can save a product, the corresponding category object must have been persisted to the database. The following code would work:

```
var category = new Category { Name = "Beverages" };
var product = new Product { Name = "Milk", Category = category };
session.Save(category);
session.Save(product);
```

The session object can also be used to delete an existing object from the database. The command to do so is as simple as the following code:

```
session.Delete(category);
```

Here, the category object we pass as a parameter to the delete method corresponds to the one we want to remove from the database.

A First Complete Sample

Time for action – Adding a new category to the database

We want to add the possibility to add a new category to the main window of our application. For this we need two textboxes where the user can enter the category name and description, we also need a button to trigger the creation of the category.

1. Add another row to the grid of the `MainWindow`; set the row height to `*`. This will be the fourth row so far. In this row, we define another grid called `CategoryGrid`, which will contain all the controls we need to create a new category. This new grid should look similar to the following code snippet:

    ```
    <Grid x:Name = "CategoryGrid" Grid.Row="3" Margin="0 10 0 0">
      <Grid.ColumnDefinitions>
        <ColumnDefinition Width="Auto"/>
        <ColumnDefinition Width="*"/>
      </Grid.ColumnDefinitions>
      <Grid.RowDefinitions>
        <RowDefinition Height="Auto" />
        <RowDefinition Height="Auto" />
        <RowDefinition Height="Auto" />
        <RowDefinition Height="*" />
      </Grid.RowDefinitions>
      <TextBlock Text="Category Name:"/>
      <TextBlock Text="Category Description:"
        Grid.Row="1"/>
      <TextBox x:Name="txtCategoryName"
        Grid.Row="0" Grid.Column="1"/>
      <TextBox x:Name="txtCategoryDescription"
        Grid.Row="1" Grid.Column="1"/>
      <Button x:Name="btnAddCategory"
        Content="Add Category"
        Grid.Row="2"
        Click="btnAddCategory_Click" />
    </Grid>
    ```

2. In the preceding code file of `MainWindow`, add the following code to the click event handler of the new button:

    ```
    private void btnAddCategory_Click(object sender,
        RoutedEventArgs e)
    {
      var factory = CreateSessionFactory();
      using (var session = factory.OpenSession())
      {
        var category = new Category
        {
    ```

[34]

```
                Name = txtCategoryName.Text,
                Description = txtCategoryDescription.Text
            };
            session.Save(category);
        }
    }
```

3. Start the application and try to add several new categories to the database. Use SSMS to verify that the categories are indeed added to the **Category** table, as shown in the following screenshot:

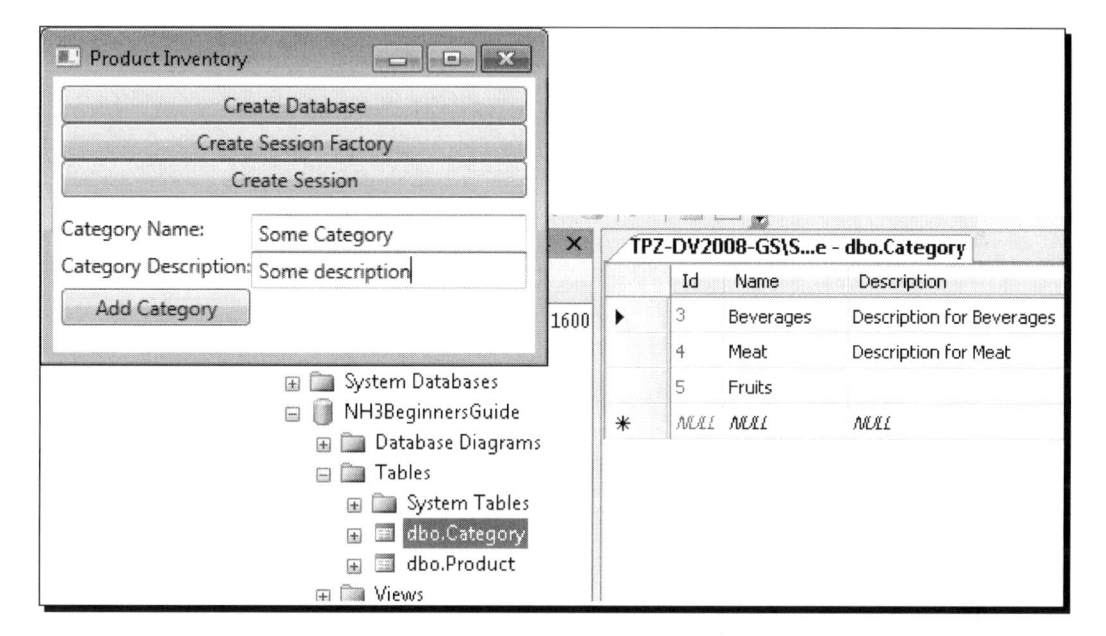

What just happened?

In this exercise, we extended our main window to be able to enter a name and description for a category, which we can then store in the database by clicking on the **Add Category** button, which we also added to the window. In the click event handler of the **Add Category** button, we implemented a code to open an NHibernate session object, create a new `Category` entity from the values entered by the user into the `Name` and `Description` textboxes, and then, using the session object, save the category to the database.

A First Complete Sample

Reading from the database

Persisting data into a database is surely important, but we also want to be able to reuse this data and thus must have a means to access it. The NHibernate session object provides us with this possibility. We can use the session object directly to access a single object in the database, which is identified by its primary key by using the following code:

```
var category = session.Get<Category>(1);
```

NHibernate will query the database for a category record in the category table having an ID of 1. NHibernate will then take this data and create a category object from it. We also say, "NHibernate rehydrates an object".

If we want to read not only a single object, but a list of objects from the database, we can use the LINQ to NHibernate provider to do so. The following statement will read all records from the category table and generate a list of the category objects out of it:

```
var categories = session.Query<Category>();
```

We can even go a step further and, for example, query a list of all discontinued products sorted by their name with the following statement:

```
var products = session.Query<Product>()
  .Where(p =>p.Discontinued)
  .OrderBy(p =>p.Name);
```

Time for action – Loading the list of all categories from the database

We want to add a list box to our application where we can display the list of all the categories that have been added to the database so far.

1. Add another row to the `CategoryGrid`. In the first column of the new row, add a command button which we will use to trigger the loading of the category list. In the second column, we need to add a list box which will be used to display the list of the retrieved categories. The XAML fragment for the button and the list box should look similar to the following code snippet:

    ```
    <Button x:Name="btnLoadCategories"
      Content="Load Categories"
      Grid.Row="3" VerticalAlignment="Top"
      Click="btnLoadCategories_Click" />
    <ListBox x:Name="lstCategories"
      Grid.Row="3" Grid.Column="1"/>
    ```

2. Add a `using NHibernate.Linq` and `using System.Linq` statement to the top of the file.

3. Now, add a code that creates a session factory, opens a new session, and loads the ordered list of categories to the click event handler of the new button. Take the list of categories and bind it to the list box. Your code should look similar to the following code snippet:

```
private void btnLoadCategories_Click(object sender,
   RoutedEventArgs e)
{
  var factory = CreateSessionFactory();
  using (var session = factory.OpenSession())
  {
    var categories = session.Query<Category>()
      .OrderBy(c =>c.Name)
      .ToList();
    lstCategories.ItemsSource = categories;
    lstCategories.DisplayMemberPath = "Name";
  }
}
```

4. Run the application and try to load the list of categories. Add more categories and then reload the list. Verify that all categories are loaded and that they are sorted by name in ascending order, as shown in the following screenshot:

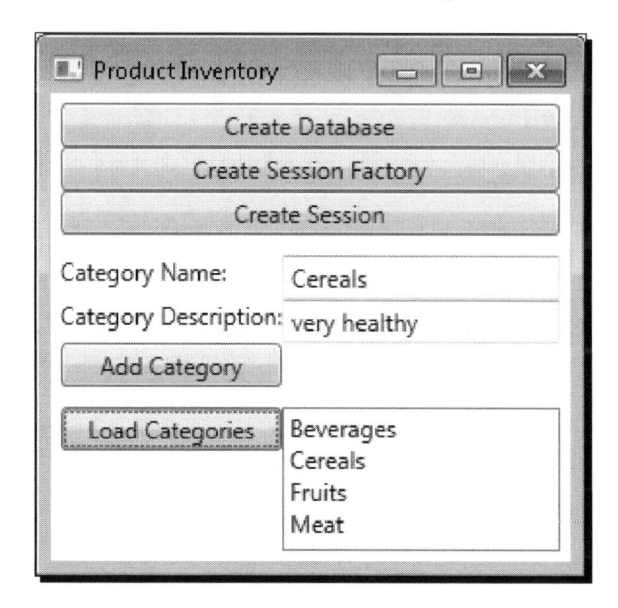

A First Complete Sample

What just happened?

We added another button, called **Load Categories**, to the main window. The code we implemented in the click event handler of this latest button opens a session object and uses a LINQ query to retrieve a list of all the categories stored so far in the database. The list is ordered by the category name and displayed in a list box, which we also added to the main window.

Have a go hero

Similar to what we have done to be able to add new categories to the database, add the necessary controls to the main window of the application, which will allow you to define a new product, and then store it in the database. It should be possible to define at least the `Name`, `UnitPrice`, and `ReorderLevel` of the product. Add an **Add Product** button to the window and in its click event handler, add the code to open a session, create a product with the data entered by the user, and store the product in the database by using the session object.

Doing the same without NHibernate – using ADO.NET only

So far, we have seen that we can, with minimal effort, write an object-oriented application which can persist its data to a RDBMS and can also recreate objects by reading previously persisted data from the RDBMS. At no time did we have to deal with any specifics of the RDBMS we chose as our data store.

If we had decided not to use an ORM framework and handcraft our data access layer, then we would have had to implement a considerable amount of code. We would also be required to have created the database schema from hand and write SQL statements for insert, update, delete, and read operations. For the C# compiler, these SQL statements are just strings and no syntax checking is possible.

Using datasets and code generation might seem to diminish the problem, but this is not a real solution. On one hand, using datasets instead of domain objects makes it more difficult to write object-oriented, extendable, scalable, and robust applications. On the other hand, code generation just covers a problem, but does not solve it. We have to get rid of the repetitive code that adds no value to our business domain and just increases the maintenance overhead.

Pop quiz

1. Instances of which of the following NHibernate classes are needed to automatically drop and re-create a database schema which corresponds to the domain model of our application:

    a. Session

    b. Configuration

    c. SchemaExport

    d. SessionFactory

    e. All of the above

Summary

We learned in this chapter what the minimal steps are that are needed to create a working application which uses NHibernate as an ORM framework, and is able to write data to and read data from a database.

Specifically, we covered:

- What the prerequisites are and how we need to configure our system to be able to develop applications that use NHibernate 3
- How we can define a model and map this model to the underlying database by using Fluent NHibernate
- How to make NHibernate automatically create a database schema for us
- How we create a session factory and how to use this factory to create sessions, which in turn are used to persist data to and retrieve the existing data from the database

Now that we've learned how we can use NHibernate in a real world application, we're ready to dig deeper into the details of the various steps we presented. In the next chapter, we start with the definition of the model.

3
Creating a Model

So far we have learned what NHibernate is and how we can implement a simple solution based on the NHibernate ORM framework. To be able to create a solution for a business domain we might not be subject matter experts of, we need to first get a deeper insight and understanding of the domain context at hand. This is where the model comes into play.

In this chapter, we shall define:

- What a model is
- What the key elements of a model are
- How we create a model

Now, let's start with some background.

What is a model

When we get the task of writing an application for a customer, we have to write a piece of software which helps our customer to automate certain aspects of their business. To be able to do this, we need to get an understanding of the business domain our customer is working in. Each business domain is different, even though there do exist some similarities. A closer look at the supposed similarities will show us that there are always important details that clearly differentiate the two business domains even in those areas.

We can only develop a solution if we have a clear understanding of the business domain. However, regularly we are laymen and have never before worked in the respective domain. By no means are we subject matter experts.

Creating a Model

To obtain this necessary understanding of the domain, we might sit together with the customer or domain experts of the customer, and develop a model of their domain.

A model is an attempt to describe reality. A model is equally understandable by us developers, as by business analysts, our customers, and their subject matter experts. Thus, a model is not a UML diagram or any other very developer-centric way of describing the domain.

A model consists of elements playing an important role in the domain we describe, a description of their relationships among each other, and the relationship to the world outside of our scope.

Reality is complex, and thus each description is only very rough and often an over simplification of the truth. To make our lives simpler we try to limit the extent of what we try to describe. We call this limited view the **scope**. We only focus on certain aspects and neglect others. When we develop the application for a customer, our solution only deals with certain aspects of the business. Usually we do not have to solve all problems of the corresponding business. Again, we can limit the scope of what we are considering, and thus the definition of a model becomes simpler and more accurate.

Having a model at hand allows us to focus on the essential parts of the problem domain, instead of getting lost in the details. It also allows us to use the same language when talking to business analysts and subject matter experts.

> Note that although this is a book about NHibernate, you will not find any reference to NHibernate in this chapter. This is a positive aspect of the ORM framework; we do not have to make any compromises regarding NHibernate in our model. Our model will consist of Plain Old CLR Objects (POCO), where CLR stands for Common Language Runtime.

Model first versus data first

In the past, we have been told that the collected data is the most important asset for a company, or to put it in a more pronounced way: "the truth is in the database". Consequently, applications were built with this notion in mind. Business analysts and architects sat down, and first designed the data model. The questions they asked were: "What type of data do we have, and how are the various pieces of data related to each other?". The result of this effort was a so-called Entity Relationship Diagram (ERD).

What makes an entity, such as a Customer specific to a certain company and/or sector? It is not the fact that there is an entity Customer with various attributes, such as name and address, but the real distinction is in how this entity is used. An entity Customer has a totally different meaning in the context of a bank than it has in the context of a travel agency.

Data sitting in a data store is of no value as long as there are no processes defined about how to use and interpret this data. However, the definition of those processes and usage scenarios are part of what we call the model of the corresponding domain. It is the domain model, which is really at the heart of an application, that adds value to a business. The data and its structure follow.

Elements of a model

A model is the attempt to describe as well as possible, and as detailed as necessary, the reality of a certain domain. A model consists of various parts that we are now going to inspect in detail.

Entity

An entity is an object that is uniquely identifiable by a combination of its attributes and has a well-defined lifespan. It starts to exist at a well-defined moment in time, it can also be destroyed or terminated in such a well-defined moment in time. Often, the entity contains an ID or key attribute, which is used to uniquely identify it.

Two entities of the same type and having the same identifier are considered to be the same entity.

In a model, we call those types of objects **entity**, whose identity and life cycle is of importance. Some typical entities in the line of business (LOB) applications are: customer, product, order, supplier, and so on. Taking an e-commerce application as an example, it is very important to be able to distinguish customers by a unique identifier, and to also know when a prospect becomes a customer, or when an existing customer is inactivated or removed from the list of customers.

As part of a model, entities play a key role. They represent important concepts of the business domain.

In real life, we are used to dealing with entities that have human readable or understandable identifiers. Such identifiers are also called **natural keys**. Typical examples are: the social security number (SSN) for US citizens, the product code for products, the account number for bank accounts, the order number for orders, and so on.

It is important to use artificial identifiers to uniquely identify entities in an application. Such artificial identifiers are also called **surrogate keys**. Another definition for this identifier is the persistent object identifier (POI). In practice, we need something to uniquely identify an instance of an entity inside a data store, like the way we can identify an instance of an entity by memory through its reference.

Why should we do this and why can't we just use the natural keys? We all know that, in real life, it can happen that a natural key has to change for one reason or the other. A product receives a new product code or a SSN has to be re-emitted. However, in an application, we need identifiers that remain the same during the whole life span of an entity, under all conditions. This can be guaranteed by using surrogate keys.

Value object

In a model, objects may exist with a life span of no interest and which do not need to be uniquely identified by an ID or a key. These kinds of objects are called **value objects**. Two instances of a value object of the same type are said to be the same if all of their properties are the same.

As a direct consequence of the above definition of a value object, it follows that value objects are immutable; that is, once a value object is defined, it cannot change anymore.

While in a banking application, an account is an entity and needs to be uniquely identified by an ID, there exists the concept of **money**, which is an object that is a combination of a value and a currency symbol. Such a money object is a good sample of a value object. Two such money objects that have the same numeric value and the same currency symbol are the same. There is no distinction between them. One object can be replaced by the other without introducing any side effects.

Other examples of value objects are:

- Name of, for example, a person entity. The Name value object consists of the surname, given name, and middle name of a person object.
- Geographical coordinate in a GIS application. Such value objects consist of a value pair for latitude and longitude.
- Color in a colorimetry application. A color object consists of values for red, green, blue, and alpha channels.
- Address in a customer relationship management (CRM) application as part of a customer entity. An address object might contain values for address line 1 and 2, zip code, and city.

Value objects never live alone. In a model, they are always part of an entity. As mentioned previously, a bank account has a balance property, which is of type money.

Time for action – Creating a Name value object

We want to create the implementation for a simple value object, we shall do so in the following example.

1. In Visual Studio, create a new project. Select **Class Library** as the template and call this project **OrderingSystem**.

2. Remove the class `Class1.cs`, that has been added by default, from the project.

3. Add a folder called `Domain` to the project.

4. Add a new class to the folder `Domain` of the project; call this class `Name`. As shown in the following code snippet:

   ```
   namespace OrderingSystem.Domain
   {
     public class Name
     { }
   }
   ```

5. Add an auto-property `LastName` of type `string` to the class. Define the setter to be `private`, as shown in the following line of code:

   ```
   public string LastName { get; private set; }
   ```

6. Add another auto-property `FirstName` of type `string` to the class. Also, define the setter to `private`. Do the same for a third and final property `MiddleName`. As shown in the following code snippet:

   ```
   public string FirstName { get; private set; }
   public string MiddleName { get; private set; }
   ```

7. Add a constructor with the three parameters `firstName`, `middleName`, and `lastName` (all of type `string`). Assign the parameters to their respective properties. Do not allow null values to be passed for `firstName` and `lastName`; if a null value is passed, then throw a descriptive exception. Your code should now look similar to the following code snippet:

   ```
   public Name(string firstName, string middleName, string lastName)
   {
     if(string.IsNullOrWhiteSpace(firstName))
       throw new ArgumentException("First name must be defined.");
     if(string.IsNullOrWhiteSpace(lastName))
       throw new ArgumentException("Last name must be defined.");

     FirstName = firstName;
     MiddleName = middleName;
     LastName = lastName;
   }
   ```

Creating a Model

8. Override the method `GetHashCode` and return a value which is a combination of the hash codes of the three individual properties. Please consult the following link: http://msdn.microsoft.com/en-us/library/system.object.gethashcode.aspx, to get an detailed description of how to construct hash codes. Please note that if `MiddleName` is equal to `null`, then we take the value zero as its hash code. Your code should look similar to the following code snippet:

```
public override int GetHashCode()
{
  unchecked
  {
    var result = FirstName.GetHashCode();
    result = (result*397) ^ (MiddleName != null ?
      MiddleName.GetHashCode() : 0);
    result = (result*397) ^ LastName.GetHashCode();
    return result;
  }
}
```

9. To be complete we now have to override the `Equals` method, which accepts one parameter of type `object`. However, first we want to add an `Equals` method that accepts a parameter of type `Name`. In this method, we do three steps:

    1. We check whether the passed parameter is `null`. If yes, then this entity and the one we compare to are not equal, and we return `false`.
    2. Then, we check whether this and the other entity are the same instance. If yes, then we return `true`.
    3. Finally, we compare each property individually. If all property values match, then we return `true`, else we return `false`. As shown in the following code snippet:

        ```
        public bool Equals(Name other)
        {
          if (other == null) return false;
          if (ReferenceEquals(this, other)) return true;
          return Equals(other.FirstName, FirstName) &&
            Equals(other.MiddleName, MiddleName) &&
            Equals(other.LastName, LastName);
        }
        ```

> Implementing an `Equals` method, whose parameter is of the same type as the class itself, corresponds to the implementation of the `IEquatable<T>` interface.

10. Now override the method `Equals` and just forward the call to the previous overload of the method (do not forget to type cast the parameter):

```
public override bool Equals(object other)
{
   return Equals(other as Name);
}
```

Congratulations. You successfully implemented your first value object type. The class diagram is as shown in the following screenshot:

Name
Class

Properties
- FirstName
- LastName
- MiddleName

Methods
- Equals (+ 1 overload)
- GetHashCode
- Name (+ 1 overload)
- operator !=
- operator ==

What just happened?

In the preceding exercise, we created a value object. We have chosen the `Name` object as an example. The properties are the first, middle, and last name of a person. To guarantee that the `Name` object is truly an immutable object, its property values can only be set through the constructor. We have also implemented the `Equals` and `GetHashCode` methods of the `Name` object, so that the two instances of this value object can be compared.

Creating an entity

We have identified various aspects that make up an entity. First of all, it is the ID which uniquely identifies and distinguishes it from another entity of the same type. Secondly, it is the attributes or properties that further describe the characteristics of an entity, and finally, it is the logic that describes the behavior of an entity.

Creating a Model

Time for action – Creating a base entity

First, we want to implement a base class for all types of entities. This class implements the logic around the ID which is common for all types of entities.

1. Add a new class to the folder `Domain` of the project and call it `Entity`. Make the class `abstract` and generic in `T`. Your code should look similar to the following code snippet:

   ```
   using System;

   namespace OrderingSystem.Domain
   {
     public abstract class Entity<T> where T : Entity<T>
     { }
   }
   ```

2. Add an auto-property `ID` of type `Guid` to the class. Make the setter of the property `private`. This will be our unique identifier for the entity. For a new entity, the `ID` will automatically have assigned the value of `Guid.Empty`, as shown in the following line of code:

   ```
   public Guid ID { get; private set; }
   ```

   > The `ID` property should have a private setter as we are never going to assign a value to `ID` through our application code. The value of `ID` is set by NHibernate through reflection at the moment the entity becomes persistent.

3. Override the `Equals` method of the class. The code should deal with the following three cases:

   1. The other entity (to which we compare this entity) is not of the same type, in which case the entities are not the same and we simply return `false`.
   2. Both this entity and the other entity are new objects and have not yet been saved in the database. In this case, we consider the two objects to be the same entity, only if they point to the same instance in memory, or in .NET terminology, if their references are equal.

3. If the two entities we compare are of the same type and are not new, then we simply have to compare their IDs and find out whether they are equal or not. As shown in the following code snippet:

```
public override bool Equals(object obj)
{
  var other = obj as T;
  if (other == null) return false;

  var thisIsNew = Equals(ID, Guid.Empty);
  var otherIsNew = Equals(other.ID, Guid.Empty);

  if (thisIsNew && otherIsNew)
    return ReferenceEquals(this, other);

  return ID.Equals(other.ID);
}
```

> Entities that have never been saved to a database are called **transient**. Entities that have been saved to the database are called **persistent**.

4. Whenever we override the `Equals` method, we also have to provide an implementation for the `GetHashCode` method. In this method, we have to just return the hash code of `ID`. Wait a second! There is a special case which we have to treat separately. This case results from the fact that an entity should never change its hash code as long as it is in memory. It is the case where the entity has been a new entity with an undefined ID and someone (for example, a HashSet<T> or Dictionary<K,T>, to which the entity has been added) has asked for its hash code. Later, this entity will be given an ID (most probably because it will be saved to the database and the data access layer will be assigning a value to the ID property). In this case, the entity can now not just return the hash code of the ID, but has to return the hash code that was calculated when it was still a new entity with an undefined ID. Considering this special case, our code should now look similar to the following code snippet:

```
private int? oldHashCode;

public override int GetHashCode()
{
  // once we have a hashcode we'll never change it
  if (oldHashCode.HasValue)
    return oldHashCode.Value;
```

Creating a Model

```
        // when this instance is new we use the base hash code
        // and remember it, so an instance can NEVER change its
        // hash code.
        var thisIsNew = Equals(ID, Guid.Empty);
        if(thisIsNew)
        {
          oldHashCode = base.GetHashCode();
          return oldHashCode.Value;
        }

        return ID.GetHashCode();
    }
```

5. Finally, we override the `==` and the `!=` operators, such that we can compare two entities without having to use the `Equals` method. Internally, both methods just use the `Equals` method:

   ```
   public static bool operator ==(Entity<T> lhs, Entity<T> rhs)
   {
     return Equals(lhs, rhs);
   }

   public static bool operator !=(Entity<T> lhs, Entity<T> rhs)
   {
     return !Equals(lhs, rhs);
   }
   ```

What just happened?

We have implemented a class that can be used as a base class for all the entities of our application. This class implements the `ID` property and the logic to use this ID to compare two instances of the same type of entity and determine whether they are equal or not. The code we have implemented is robust and deals with all possible edge cases.

Time for action – Creating a Customer entity

Now, let's implement a real entity that inherits from the base entity. Here we can focus fully on the properties that describe the entity and on the methods that describe the entity's behavior.

1. Add a new class to the folder `Domain` of the project and call this class `Customer`.

2. Make the `Customer` entity inherit from the `Entity` base class.

   ```
   public class Customer : Entity<Customer>
   { }
   ```

3. In the class `Customer`, implement the following auto-properties: `CustomerIdentifier` of type `string` and `CustomerName` of type `Name`. Make the setters of the properties `private`, as shown in the following code snippet:

```
public string CustomerIdentifier { get; private set; }
public Name CustomerName { get; private set; }
```

4. Implement a method `ChangeCustomerName` with the values: `firstName`, `middleName`, and `lastName` as parameters. The method changes the `CustomerName` property of the class. The code looks similar to the following code snippet:

```
public void ChangeCustomerName(string firstName, string
   middleName, string lastName)
{
   CustomerName = new Name(firstName, middleName, lastName);
}
```

5. In the following screenshot, we see a class diagram of the **Customer** entity we just implemented, together with its base class and the `Name` value object, which is used as a type of the `CustomerIdentifier` property of the `Customer` class.

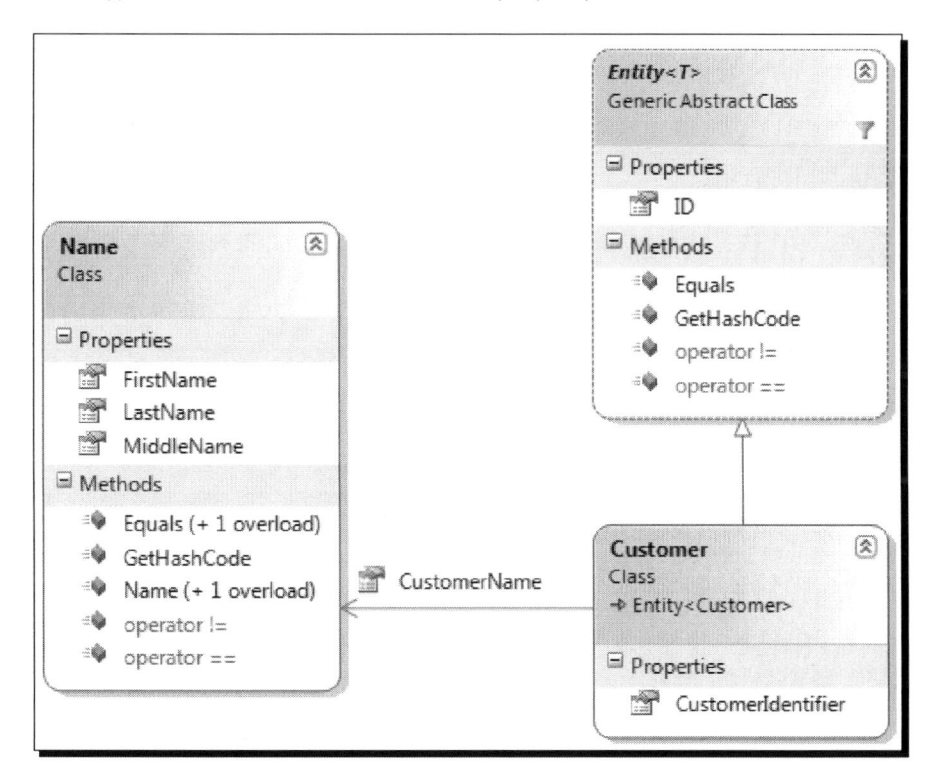

What just happened?

We have implemented our first entity. The **Customer** entity we implemented inherits from the `Entity<T>` base class we implemented in the preceding exercise. We also used the `Name` value object we defined earlier as the type of one of the `Customer`'s properties.

Defining relations between entities

Entities are one of the key concepts of a model. However, entities do not live in isolation; they are related to other entities. We can distinguish between different types of relations.

Owns or contains

Value objects can never exist alone. They only become a meaning in conjunction with an entity. An entity can own or contain zero to many value objects. In the case of the previous `Customer` entity, the value object `Name` is owned or contained by the `Customer` entity. This relation is indicted by an arrow pointing from the entity to the value object, as shown in the following screenshot. Near to the arrow head, we find the name of the value object type property in the entity.

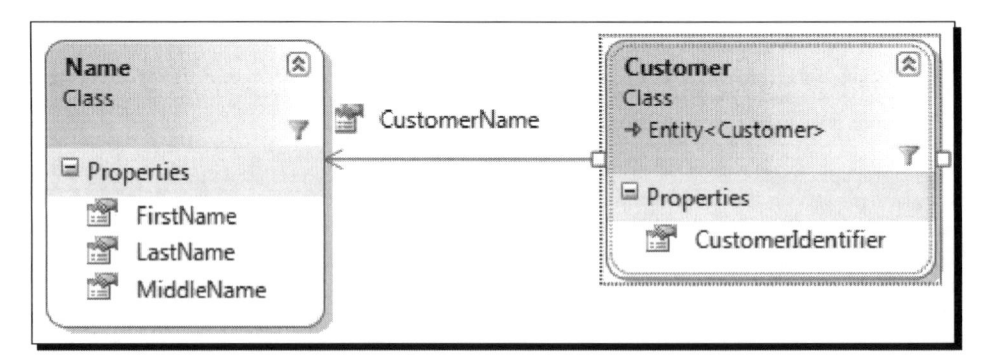

Note that there is no arrow pointing back from **Name** to **Customer**. The `Name` value object does not and should not know its owner.

If we look at the code, then the relation is defined by implementing a property of type `Name` in the `Customer` class, as shown in the following code snippet:

```
public Name CustomerName { get; private set; }
```

One-to-many

Let's now look at the two entities, `Product` and `Category`, we introduced in Chapter 2. How are they related to each other?

- Each product belongs to exactly one category. We can thus define a property `Category` of type `Category` in the `Product` class. This property is said to be a reference to the category of the product. It can be used to navigate from the product to its associated category. This relation between product and category is marked with an arrow pointing from **Product** to **Category** in the following screenshot. The name (**Category**) of the property, which can be used to navigate from **Product** to **Category**, is marked near the arrow head. The code would look similar to the following code snippet:

    ```
    public Category Category { get; private set; }
    ```

- Each category has many associated products. Consequently, we can define a `Products` property in the `Category` class, which is a collection or set of products. This relation is marked with a double-headed arrow pointing from **Category** to **Product**, as shown in the following screenshot. Again, the name of the property (**Products**) that is used to navigate from the **Category** to its associated products is marked near the arrow head. Here, the code might look similar to the following code snippet:

    ```
    private List<Products> products;
    public IEnumerable<Product> Products { get { return products; } }
    ```

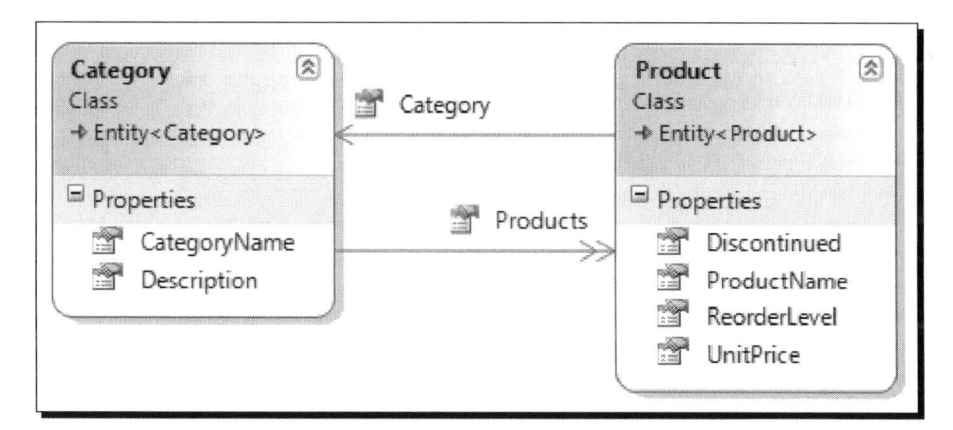

![Category and Product class diagram]

> In a real life inventory application, you will probably want to avoid putting a `Products` collection on the `Category` entity, as it is possible that a category can have hundreds, if not thousands, of associated products. To load the whole, huge collection of products for a given category would be unwise and would lead to an application having unsatisfactory response times.

Creating a Model

One-to-one

Sometimes, we encounter the situation where an entity acts in different roles. As an example, take a **Person** entity, which at a university can wear different hats. One and the same **Person** can work as **Professor** in a faculty of the university, but at the same time, can also be a **Student** in a different faculty. Such a relationship can be modeled as a one-to-one relationship.

Another one-to-one relationship in the same domain would be the one between **Professor** and his possible role as **HeadOfDepartment**.

In the following screenshot, we see a class diagram of the entities and the relationships mentioned previously.

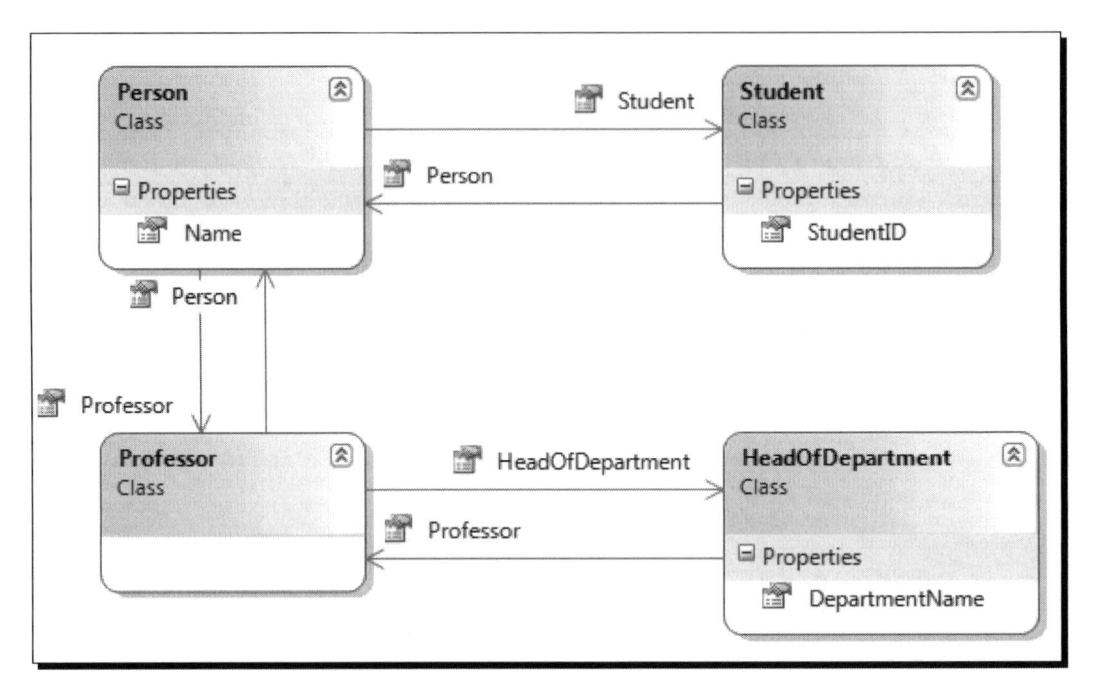

Note that we can navigate from a **Person** object to its associated **Professor** object through the property **Professor**. We can also navigate from a professor object to the corresponding person object via the property **Person** of the professor entity. This is indicated by the two arrows in the preceding screenshot, one pointing from the **Person** to the **Professor** and the other pointing in the opposite direction.

In a similar way, we can navigate from **Person** to **Student** and back, as well as from **Professor** to **HeadOfDepartment** and back.

Many-to-many

The last type of relation we want to discuss is a many-to-many relation. What does this mean? Let's look at a concrete example: the relation between an order and a product. A customer wants to order a product. However, the customer does not want to order only one product, but several different products. Thus, an order can contain many products. On the other hand, several different customers can place orders for one and the same product. Therefore, a product can belong to many orders. Another example would be the relation between a book and an author. An author can write many different books, while a book can have many authors. Both of these relations are examples for a many-to-many relationship, as shown in the following screenshot:

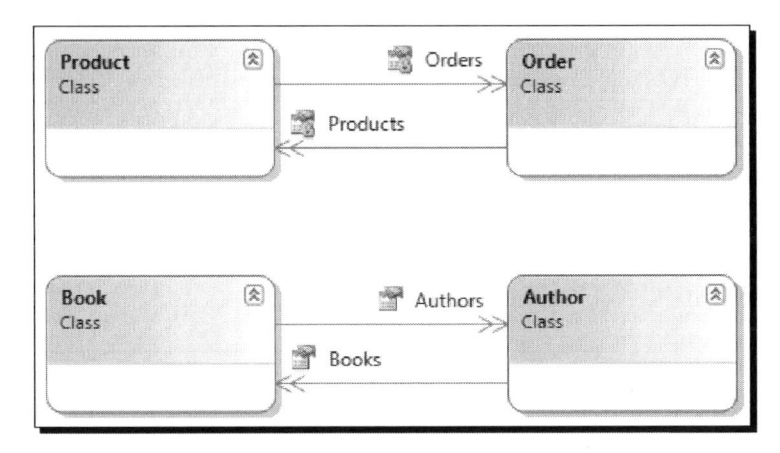

However, there are subtle differences between the two. We can leave the latter relationship as it is; it is a real many-to-many relation. Nevertheless, we need to discuss the relation between product and order a little more. Thinking a bit more about the process of placing orders, we will realize that there is some concept missing. A customer might not only want to order one unit of a product, but maybe several. Also, we might want to know the unit price of the product at the time when the order was placed and the discount applicable to the specific product. All of a sudden, a new intermediate entity (a relational entity – it relates product and order) is born. We often call this intermediate entity a line item of an order. We can change our diagram and make it look similar to the following screenshot:

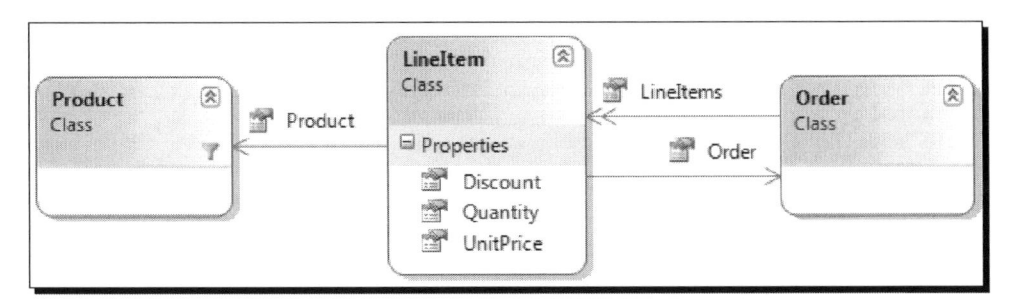

Creating a Model

Evidently, we have no more many-to-many relations in this part of the model, but rather reference type and one-to-many relations. Specifically, an order has many line items and each line item references a product.

The order entry model

Now that we have discussed in detail all the elements comprising a model, it is time to implement a simple yet realistic and complete example domain model. This model shall provide us with a better understanding of the domain our Customer, for which we built the application, works in.

Time for action – Implementing an order entry model

The context of the model is an order entry system. The model shall be used as a base for a solution that helps to enter orders into the system. Those orders are placed by customers via phone calls.

1. Take a piece of paper and try to identify entities that play a role in this context. Draw a box for each entity identified. Try to come up with a solution without reading ahead!

2. Define the relations between the entities by drawing connecting lines between them. Try to define the type of relation, whether it is a one-to-many, or a reference, and so on.

3. For each entity, define and write in the corresponding box the most important properties.

4. Try to identify sets of properties in your entities that are good candidates for value objects.

5. You should have come up with a model that looks similar to the following screenshot.

> Note: to keep things manageable, the model only shows a very simplified version of an order entry system. In reality, the domain would have many more entities and the entities themselves would have additional properties not shown here.

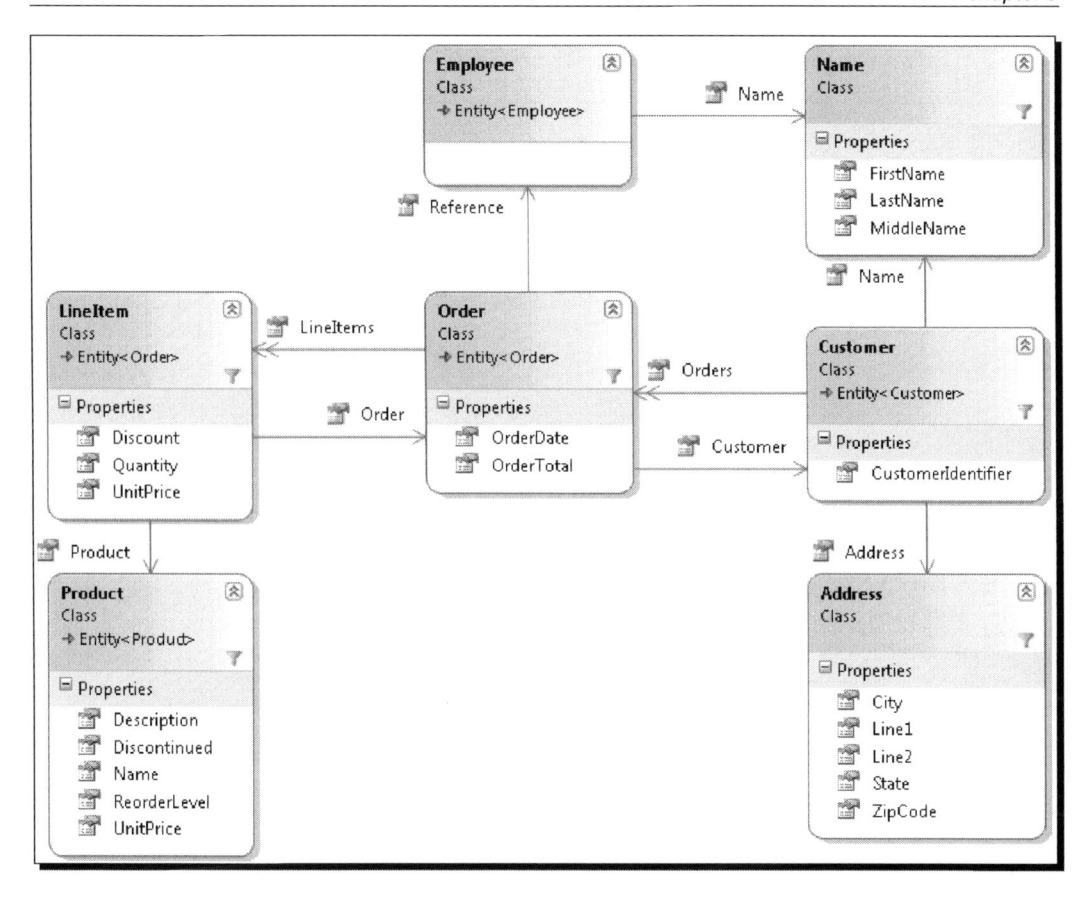

6. In Visual Studio, open the solution **OrderingSystem**.

7. First, we create the value objects we identified in the model.

    a. We have already defined the class `Name`, which is a value object and consists of the three properties: `LastName`, `FirstName`, and `MiddleName`. (Both the `Employee` and the `Customer` entities have a property of type `Name`.)

    b. Add a class `Address` to the `Domain` folder of the project and add the following properties to it (all of type string): `Line1`, `Line2`, `ZipCode`, `City`, and `State`. Override the `Equals` and `GetHashCode` methods as we did in the `Name` class. The code should look similar to the following code snippet:

    ```
    public bool Equals(Address other)
    {
        if (other == null) return false;
    ```

Creating a Model

```
      if (ReferenceEquals(this, other)) return true;
      return Equals(other.Line1, Line1) &&
        Equals(other.Line2, Line2) &&
        Equals(other.ZipCode, ZipCode) &&
        Equals(other.City, City) &&
        Equals(other.State, State);
    }

    public override bool Equals(object obj)
    {
      return Equals(obj as Address);
    }

    public override int GetHashCode()
    {
      unchecked
      {
        var result = Line1.GetHashCode();
        result = (result * 397) ^ (Line2 != null ?
          Line2.GetHashCode() : 0);
        result = (result * 397) ^ ZipCode.GetHashCode();
        result = (result * 397) ^ City.GetHashCode();
        result = (result * 397) ^ State.GetHashCode();
        return result;
      }
    }
}
```

8. We have already defined the class `Entity<TEntity>` in the project and will use this class as the base class for all the other entities we are going to add to the model.

9. Now, let's add a class for each entity to the project. Each of these classes inherits from `Entity<TEntity>`:

    a. To the `Domain` folder add a class `Employee`, which inherits from `Entity<Employee>`.

    b. We have already added a class `Customer`, which inherits from the `Entity<Customer>` earlier in this chapter; thus nothing to do here.

    c. To the `Domain` folder add a class `Order`, which inherits from `Entity<Order>`.

    d. To the `Domain` folder add a class `LineItem`, which inherits from `Entity<LineItem>`.

    e. To the `Domain` folder add a class `Product`, which inherits from `Entity<Product>`.

10. Add a property `Name` of type `Name` to the `Employee` class.

11. Add an additional property `Address` of type `Address` to the `Customer` class.

12. Also, add a read-only collection of `Orders` to the `Customer` class, as shown in the following code snippet:

```
private readonly List<Order> orders;
public IEnumerable<Order> Orders { get { return orders; } }
```

13. Add properties `Customer` of type `Customer`, `Reference` of type `Employee`, `OrderDate` of type `DateTime`, and `OrderTotal` of type `decimal` to the `Order` class.

14. Add a read-only collection of `LineItems` to the `Order` class, as shown in the following code snippet:

```
private readonly List<LineItem> lineItems;
public IEnumerable<LineItem> LineItems
{ get { return lineItems; } }
```

15. Add a constructor as shown in the following code snippet to the `Order` class:

```
public Order(Customer customer)
{
   lineItems = new List<LineItem>();
   Customer = customer;
   OrderDate = DateTime.Now;
}
```

16. Add properties `Order` (`Order`), `Product` (`Product`), `Quantity` (`int`), `UnitPrice` (`decimal`), and `Discount` (`decimal`) to the `LineItem` class.

17. Now, add a constructor to the `LineItem` class, which initializes its properties with values passed in (specifically, note how `UnitPrice` and `Discount` are initialized):

```
public LineItem(Order order, int quantity, Product product)
{
   Order = order;
   Quantity = quantity;
   Product = product;
   UnitPrice = product.UnitPrice;

   if (quantity >= 10)
      Discount = 0.05m;
}
```

Creating a Model

18. Add the properties `Name` (string), `Description` (string), `UnitPrice` (decimal), `ReorderLevel` (int), and `Discontinued` (bool) to the `Product` class.

    Now we have defined our domain entities, their relations among each other, as well as their properties. The result of our implementation is what we call an **anemic domain model** as it contains no business logic and the entities are mere data containers.

    Let's add some logic to the entities. We want to implement the user story "place order for existing customer". A Customer orders several different products. Of each product, they order several items.

    The preceding user story can result in a command that is sent from the user interface of our application to the domain model. The command contains a list of `LineInfo` objects that each contain the number of items and the ID of the product that the Customer ordered.

19. Add a class `LineInfo` to the folder `Domain` of the project. This class will be used as a data transfer object (DTO) and is defined as shown in the following code snippet:

    ```
    public class LineInfo
    {
      public int ProductId { get; set; }
      public int Quantity { get; set; }
    }
    ```

20. Let's add a method `PlaceOrder` to the class `Customer`. Inside the method, we add code to create a new order and add a product to the order for each passed `LineInfo`. Our code should look similar to the following code snippet:

    ```
    public void PlaceOrder(LineInfo[] lineInfos,
        IDictionary<int, Product> products)
    {
      var order = new Order(this);
      foreach (var lineInfo in lineInfos)
      {
        var product = products[lineInfo.ProductId];
        order.AddProduct(this, product, lineInfo.Quantity);
      }
      orders.Add(order);
    }
    ```

> Note that the products dictionary that is passed in as a second parameter contains all products, which are referenced by one of the `LineInfo` items through its `ProductID`. The origin of this dictionary is not of interest in this chapter and will be discussed in a later chapter.

21. Now, we have to define the `AddProduct` method of the `Order` class. This method internally creates a new `LineItem` object and adds it to the order's line item collection, as shown in the following snippet of code:

```
public void AddProduct(Customer customer, Product product,
   int quantity)
{
   Customer = customer;
   var line = new LineItem(this, quantity, product);
   lineItems.Add(line);
}
```

What just happened?

Hurray! We have successfully defined the model for a simple order entry system. Our model contains all key elements of a typical business context model. Of course, to make our model fully functional, we would have to implement more user stories similar to the "place order" story.

Pop quiz – Identifying entities

1. An entity always has an identifier. This identifier is used to:
    a. Uniquely identify an entity.
    b. Compare two entities of the same type for equality.
    c. Both of the above.

Have a go hero – Extending the model

Try to extend the order entry model and add an `EmployeePhoto` entity, which has a one-to-one relation with the `Employee` entity and contains properties to deal with an image, the title of the image, and a short description of the image.

Summary

In this chapter, we have learned what a model is and how it helps us to better understand the domain for which we may want to implement an application. We have learned that entities and their relations among each other play a key role in a model. We discussed the notion of identity and the life cycle of an entity. Also, we have introduced the concept of value objects and pointed out its differences with the entity.

At no point did we have to reference NHibernate or make any compromises just to satisfy the needs of the NHibernate ORM framework. This is a very positive factor as it helps us to keep focused on the context and not introduce unnecessary complexity, which has nothing to do with the domain context at hand.

Last but not least, in this chapter we have also briefly contrasted the **model first** versus the **data first** approach when designing a solution.

Now we are ready to think about how we are going to persist the data that our model produces in a database. That is where NHibernate comes to play. First, we will discuss how to map our model, such that it is compatible with a relational data store. This will be the topic of the next chapter.

4
Defining the Database Schema

In this chapter, we will learn how data produced by our applications can be stored in a relational database and how this data is organized inside the database.

In this chapter, we shall:

- Learn what a table is
- Learn how tables are related to each other
- Discuss strategies to constrain what data can be stored
- Show what possibilities we have to improve the performance of the data access
- Create the `OrderingSystem` database

So let's get on with it...

What is a database schema?

Every realistic application produces and manipulates data. This data has to be stored somewhere where it can be protected from such things as power outage, or the fact that even today our computers do not have an infinite amount of memory, while the amount of data has grown to the size of terabytes or exabytes. Although many different types of data stores exist, for example, XML, document databases, Google Big Table, and so on, in this book, we want to concentrate solely on relational database management systems (RDBMS) such as Microsoft SQL Server.

In a relational database, the **database schema** is a description of the structure of the database, and as such, describes how the data is organized inside the database and is divided into database tables. The schema also contains specifications about the type of data that can be stored, the relations of the database tables among each other, and the access strategies selected when accessing the data. In a relational database, a schema defines tables, fields or columns, relationships, indexes, constraints, views, and stored procedures, among others.

Who owns the database?

The content of this book is based on the assumption that the database is owned by the application. This implicates that the database should only be manipulated by one single application, your application. No other application should have direct access to your database. Access to the data in the database for other applications has to be provided through APIs controlled by your application, for example, in the form of web services.

Given this boundary condition, we can now leverage this to our advantage:

- We can create the database schema in a way that optimally fits our domain model and we do not have to make any compromises
- We can rely on the fact that the data in the database is correct as it is only written by our application (if, on the other hand, we find that there is bad data in the database, then we know it must be due to defects in our own application)

Many people will disagree with that assumption. Why? In the past, we have been unanimously told that the truth lies in the database. There have been heroic attempts to create centralized databases that contain all data of an enterprise such as a bank. All applications that were written in the respective enterprise would access and use this central data store. Although there were very good reasons to try to implement such a central data store, the negative side effects outweighed the positive factors by far. Autonomous systems are far more flexible than centralized and strongly coupled systems.

Time for action – Creating the OrderingSystem database

In this first exercise, we want to create a brand new SQL Server database.

1. Open SQL Server Management Studio (SSMS) and log in to your SQL Server Express.

2. In the **Connect to Server** dialog, choose **Database Engine** as **Server type**. We are accessing the locally installed database server, thus enter either **.\SQLExpress** or **(local)\SQLEXPRESS** as **Server name**. Finally, select **Windows Authentication** as the **Authentication** method and click on **Connect**, as shown in the preceding screenshot.

3. You will be presented with a screen similar to the following screenshot. This shows a basic summary of the SQL Server instance that you are connected to, such as the databases on the server, security information (logins, roles), and so on.

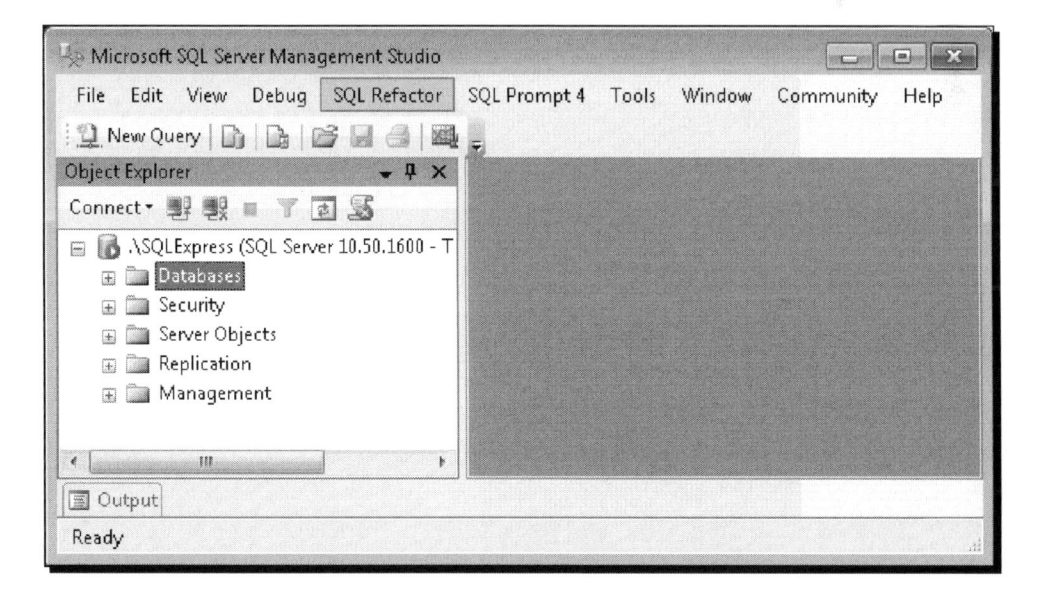

Defining the Database Schema

4. In the **Object Explorer** window, right-click on the **Databases** node and select **New Database...**.

5. In the **New Database** dialog, enter **OrderingSystem** as **Database name**, as shown in the following screenshot. Leave all other settings as their default values and click on **OK**.

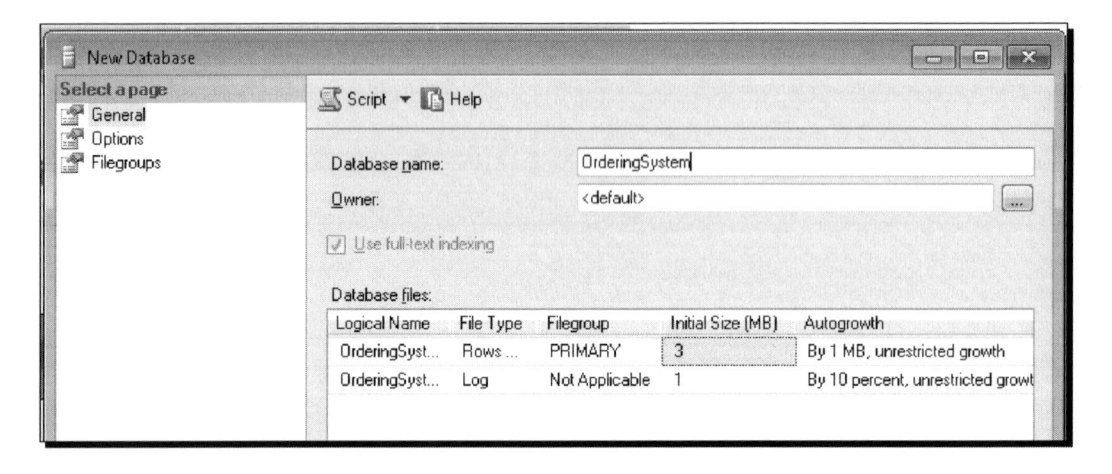

6. The newly created database appears as a sub-node of the **Databases** folder. Expand this new node and you will see several sub-nodes, as shown in the following screenshot:

7. You will see the collapsed folders for **Tables** and **Views**, as well as **Database Diagrams** and **Security**. These are the most common objects we will use within SSMS to create database objects and manage their security permissions.

What just happened?

We have just created our basic ordering system database. We will continue to use this database throughout this chapter and throughout the entire book.

Now that we have our database, we can move on to creating a structure to store our data!

Laying the foundation – table layouts

The first and foremost important element of a schema is the table. Data is stored inside tables. A table is comparable to a spreadsheet, as you might be familiar with from tools such as Microsoft Excel. It consists of a collection of rows and columns. While the rows of a table represent the actual data, the table contains the columns that define what type of data is stored in a table. In the following screenshot, we have a sample of a very simple table storing product category data:

CategoryId	Name	Description
1	Beverages	Non alcoholic liquids
2	Liquors	Strong alcoholic liquids
3	Meat	All goodness from the animal
4	Vegetable	Green stuff
NULL	NULL	NULL

The table name is **Categories**, which denotes what we also call the **database entity** we are dealing with. The column headers represent the attributes of the database entity. In this case we have **CategoryId**, **Name**, and **Description** properties.

Each row of the table contains the data of exactly one instance of a product category. Consequently, we have as many different categories as there are rows in the table.

The preceding screenshot provides the data view of a table. Also, what is interesting is the structural view of a table, as shown in the following screenshot. It shows us the metadata of the table. In this screenshot, we can see some of this metadata. We can see that:

- The table has three columns with the names **CategoryId**, **Name**, and **Description**.
- **CategoryId** has a data type of **int**, while **Name** is a Unicode character string with a maximum of 50 characters, and **Description** is also a Unicode character string but of **MAX** length. On SQL Server, MAX stands for a character string of up to 4 GB.

Defining the Database Schema

- **CategoryId** and **Name** cannot be undefined or null. **Description** is an optional bit of information, and thus there is a checkmark in the Allow Nulls column.
- **CategoryId** is the Primary Key field denoted with the small key symbol on the left-hand side.

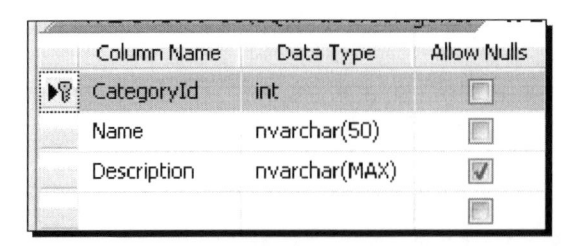

Column Name	Data Type	Allow Nulls
CategoryId	int	☐
Name	nvarchar(50)	☐
Description	nvarchar(MAX)	☑
		☐

Time for action – Creating the Categories table

In this second exercise, we want to create the first table in our **OrderingSystem** database.

1. Open SSMS and in the **Object Browser** expand the **Databases** folder. Locate the **OrderingSystem** database we created in the previous exercise and expand it.

2. Right-click on the **Tables** folder and select **New Table...**, as shown in the following screenshot:

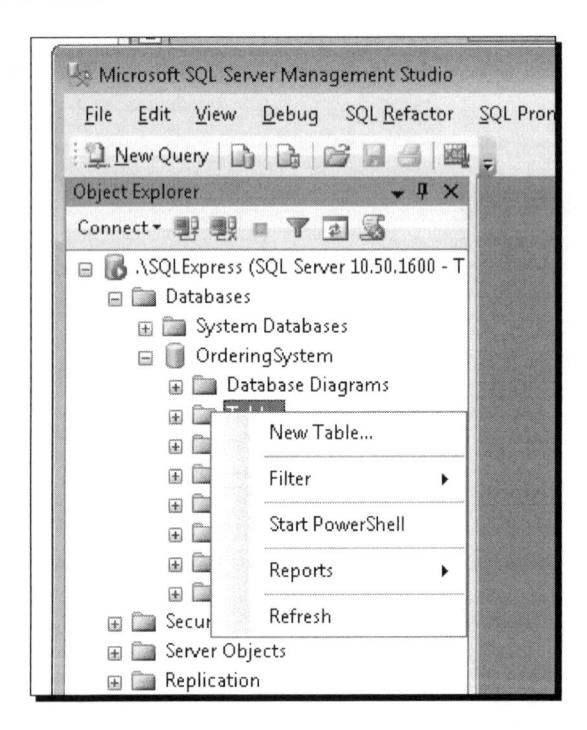

3. SSMS will open a new tab where we can now define the details of the new table. The new table editor tab will look similar to the table in the following screenshot. In the **Column Name** box, enter **Id**, either type or select **int** in the **Data Type** field, and uncheck the **Allow Nulls** checkbox.

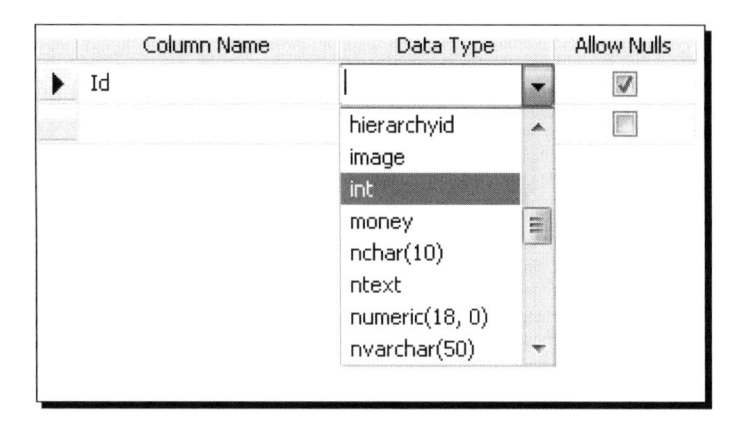

4. In the second row, add **Name** as **Column Name**, **nvarchar(50)** as **Data Type**, and also leave **Allow Nulls** unchecked.

5. Add a row for each of these:

   a. Column name **UnitPrice**, data type **money**, and **Allow Nulls** unchecked.

   b. Column name **ReorderLevel**, data type **int**, and **Allow Nulls** unchecked.

   c. Column name **Discontinued**, data type **bit**, and **Allow Nulls** unchecked.

   d. Column name **Description**, data type **nvarchar(MAX)**, and **Allow Nulls** checked, as shown in the following screenshot:

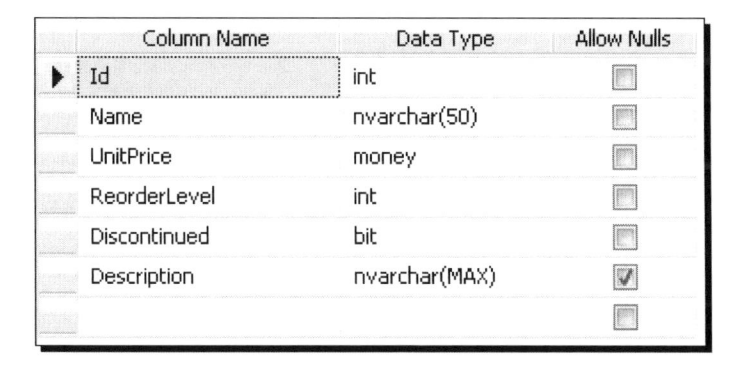

Defining the Database Schema

6. Select the first row where you have defined the **Id** column and right-click on this row, as shown in the following screenshot:

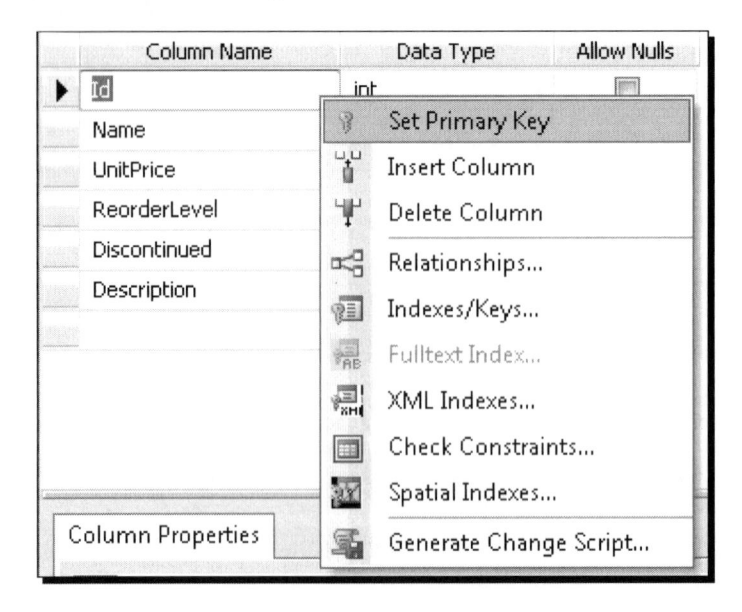

7. Select **Set Primary Key**. A small key symbol should appear left of the column name.

8. Finally, we need to save our table and give it a name. You can save the file by clicking on the Save (floppy disk) icon, pressing *Ctrl + S*, or selecting **File** | **Save Table_1**. Any of these options will bring up the **Save Table** dialog box, which will prompt us to choose a name for our table, as shown in the following screenshot:

9. Press *CTRL + S* to save the table. In the **Choose Name** dialog box, enter **Products** as the name for the new table and click on **OK**.

What just happened?

Using SSMS, we have just defined our first database table that we will use later on to store our product entities. We have used the visual designers of SSMS to define the columns of the database table and to also define which column of the table is the Primary Key.

Time for action – Defining a script to create the Products table

The database table designer comes in very handy when we want to quickly define a new table as a one-time action. However, if we want to redo the same action again and again, then defining a script is better. In this exercise, we will define a SQL DDL script which generates the product table for us.

> **DDL** is the acronym for Data Definition Language or Data Description Language and is a computer language for defining data structures such as tables. Its sister **DML**, which stands for Data Manipulation Language, is a computer language used to insert, update, and delete data in the database.

1. In your editor of choice, (I chose Notepad++, a free Notepad clone) open a new text file.

2. Enter SQL code to create a `Products` table, as shown in the following lines of code:
   ```
   create table Products( )
   GO
   ```

3. For each column we want to define for this table, add a line containing first the name of the column and then its data type. Do this for `Id` (int), `Name` (nvarchar(50)), `UnitPrice` (money), `ReorderLevel` (int), `Discontinued` (bit), and `Description` (nvarchar(MAX)).

4. If a column must be defined, then add a `NOT NULL` after the respective column type.

5. Add code to define the `Id` column to be the `primary key` of the table.

6. Your code should look similar to the following code snippet:

```sql
create table Products (
  Id int not null,
  Name nvarchar(50) not null,
  UnitPrice money not null,
  ReorderLevel int not null,
  Discontinued bit not null,
  Description nvarchar(MAX),
  primary key (Id)
  )
GO
```

7. Save the file as `0001_create_Products_table.sql`.

What just happened?

Using a simple text editor, we have created a SQL DDL script which when executed in the database creates the `Products` table for us. Creating scripts to manipulate the database schema is the preferred way over manipulating the schema with a designer such as SSMS whenever we want to repeatedly execute the same action.

Table columns

The columns of the table define what kind of information we can store in a table. If we make a comparison between a table and an entity type (a C# class), then we can say that the table column is equivalent to a property of the entity. To define a property on a class, we have to give it a name and a data type. Similarly, a table column has a name and a data type. We can define even more characteristics on a column such as a restriction whether the column is nullable or not. By the way, **null** is a database term used to define an **undefined value**.

Data types of table columns

You might have already noticed that the data types used for table columns differ quite a bit from those you generally use when defining properties of a C# class. The only column data type that looks familiar so far is **int**. This is a fact we have to live with. It is even worse as every database product has its own specific types. Oracle column types are different from those of Microsoft SQL Server, which in turn are different from the column types used by MySQL, and so on.

Luckily, NHibernate does a good job in automatically converting the data types for us from .NET types to database types and vice versa. However, it is still important to have a good understanding of those differences.

The following table lists the most common .NET types and its counterparts in MS SQL Server and in Oracle:

.NET	SQL Server	Oracle	Comment
int	int	NUMBER(p,0)	**p** is the precision and specifies the maximal number of decimal digits that can be stored.
decimal	money or decimal(p,s)	NUMBER(p,s)	**s** is the scale and specifies the maximal number of decimal digits that can be stored to the right of the decimal point.
			For example, NUMBER (7,2) has 5 digits before and 2 digits after the decimal point.
string	nvarchar(50)	VARCHAR2(50)	For short strings of up to 4000 characters. Stores Unicode characters.
string	nvarchar(MAX)	NCLOB	For strings of a length of up to 4 GB. Stores Unicode characters.
bool	bit	CHAR(1)	Oracle does not have a Boolean type. Often it is simulated by a char(1) column containing either **Y** or **N**.
DateTime	datetime	TIMESTAMP	Date and time.
DateTime	date	DATE	Date only.
byte[]	varbinary(n)	RAW	Variable length binary strings of up to 2000 bytes. **n** is the max length of the array.
byte[]	varbinary(MAX)	BLOB	Stores unstructured binary large objects of up to 4 GB.

In contradiction to the common type system of .NET, a unified type system for databases does not exist. Each database vendor or provider has its own specific type system.

Relations, constraints, and indices

So far, we have seen that a relational database allows us to organize our data into different tables. To bring even more structure to how the data is stored and what data is stored, relational databases use constraints and relations. Furthermore, we can define indexes to optimize the access of the data.

Relations

Relations are used to associate data in different tables. Only through these relations, data stored in a database has some business-relevant meaning. Otherwise, the data would just be a bunch of unrelated sets of facts. Relational databases are called relational due to this fact that the data is related among different tables.

As an example, let's look at the connection between the data of a customer and the data of orders placed by this customer. How is this relation defined in a relational database system?

For example, let's take a single customer record. This record can be considered the parent of some order records. We have a so called parent–child relation, where the order records are the children of the customer record. The customer record is uniquely identified by its Primary Key. Each child record (that is, each order record) now stores the value of its parent's Primary Key in a special column. This column is then called the **foreign key**. As a result, an order record is related to its parent via this foreign key. We can visualize this relation as follows:

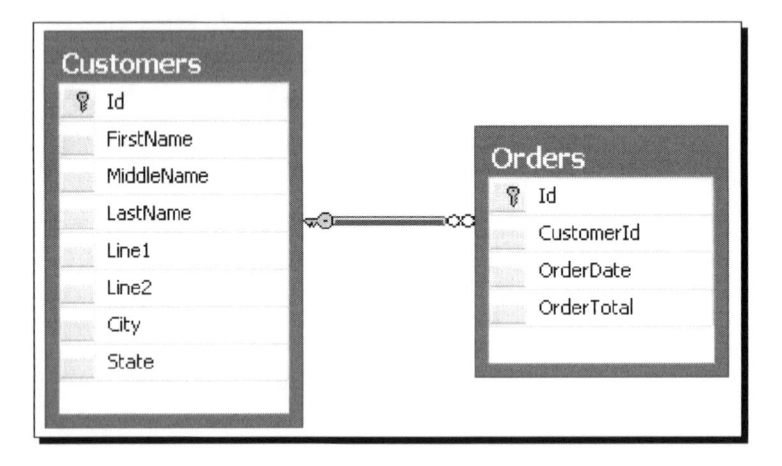

The line between the **Customers** and the **Orders** tables has a key symbol at the end pointing to the **Customers** table and an infinity symbol (∞) at the other end towards the **Orders** table. This means that the parent record which is referenced via its Primary Key is in the **Customers** table, while the child records are in the **Orders** table. The **Orders** table contains a field **CustomerId** which is used as the foreign key. The infinity symbol also indicates that there can be many order records associated with a single customer record.

There exist three types of relations in a relational database. It is the same kind of relations that we discussed in the previous chapter when we discussed the relations between entities in a model:

- **One-to-many relations**: One parent record can have zero to many associated child records. A good example for this type of relation is the **Customers** to **Orders** relation just discussed.

- **One-to-one relations**: This is a degenerated one-to-many relation where a parent record can have exactly one associated child record. Often the records having such a relation share the same Primary Key. No special foreign key field is then needed in the child table.

    A good example of such a relation is the relation between a product record and its associated product photo record. This can be visualized as shown in the following screenshot:

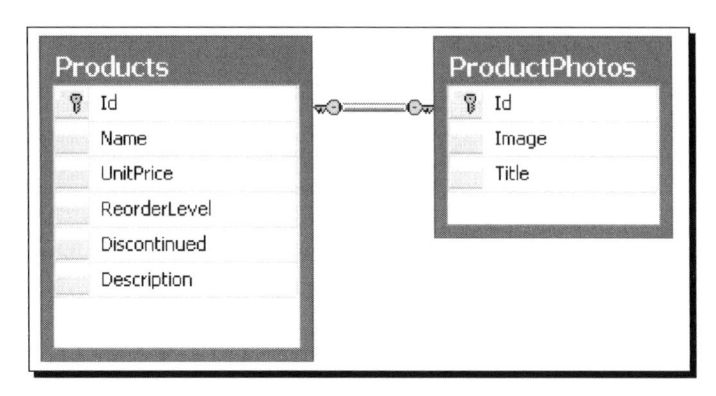

    Note the key symbol on both sides of the connecting line between **Products** and **ProductPhotos**.

- **Many-to-many relations**: A parent record can have many associated child records. Each child record in turn can have many associated parent records. The sample from the ordering system domain is the relation between orders and products. A single order can contain many products, and each product can be present in many different orders. Another familiar relation of this type is the relation between a book and an author. A book can be written by many authors and an author can write more than one book.

    To establish such a relationship, we need a helper table that mitigates between the two ends. This table is called a **relational table** and has no other purpose than to relate two database entities or tables. In the case of the order to product relation, it would be the **LineItems** table. This can be visualized as shown in the following screenshot:

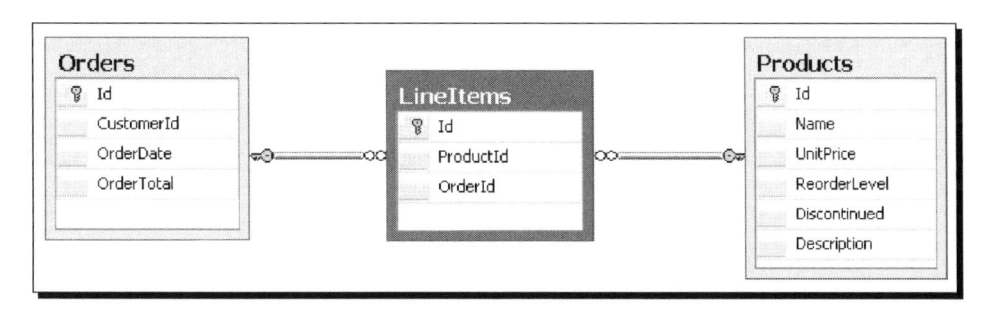

In the preceding screenshot, the ends of the lines with the key symbol are pointing towards the **Orders** and **Products** tables, indicating that those tables contain the Primary Keys. On the other hand, the **LineItems** table contains two foreign key fields: one for the **Orders (OrderId)** and one for the **Products** table (**ProductId**).

> Often, relational tables are only used to connect two other tables in a **many-to-many** relationship. In this case, those relational tables only consist of foreign keys pointing to the respective records in the tables which they connect. However, sometimes it makes sense to store some additional information in these relational tables, and thus add characteristics to a relation. One such example is **LineItems** which connects **Orders** and **Products**. Typically, we store information like **Quantity**, **Discount**, and so on in the **LineItems** table.

Constraints

Constraints are used to limit the data that can be saved in a table. Constraints are defined for a table column. Various constraints exist:

- **Not null constraints**: When storing data in a table, the value of the column that is defined as NOT NULL cannot be undefined. This constraint is useful in all situations where the existence of a value is mandatory, for example, the name of a product must be defined.

- **The data type**: The data type of a column is also a kind of constraint as it limits the possible values that the column can contain to a well-defined subset. As an example, the ReorderLevel of the product must be an integral number.

- **Check constraints**: In most modern relational databases, we can define formulas to further limit the values that can be stored in a database column. As an example, we would not want the ReorderLevel to be a negative number and can add a check constraint to avoid this.

- **Foreign key constraints**: This constraint ensures that there cannot be a foreign key of a child table pointing to a non-existing parent record in the parent table. For example, a product cannot have a foreign key CategoryId with a value of 1 if no category with Id equal to 1 exists.

Time for action – Adding a constraint to the Product table

In this exercise, we will use the table designer of SSMS to define a check constraint to the column `ReorderLevel` of the `Products` table.

1. In SSMS, locate the table **Products**, right-click on it and select **Design**. The table designer for the **Products** table opens in a new tab.

2. Inside the table designer, right-click in any column and select **Check Constraints…**. The **Check Constraints** dialog window opens.

3. Click on **Add** to add a new check constraint.

4. Change the **(Name)** to **CK_Product_ReorderLevel**.

5. In the **Expression** field, add **ReorderLevel>=0**, as shown in the following screenshot:

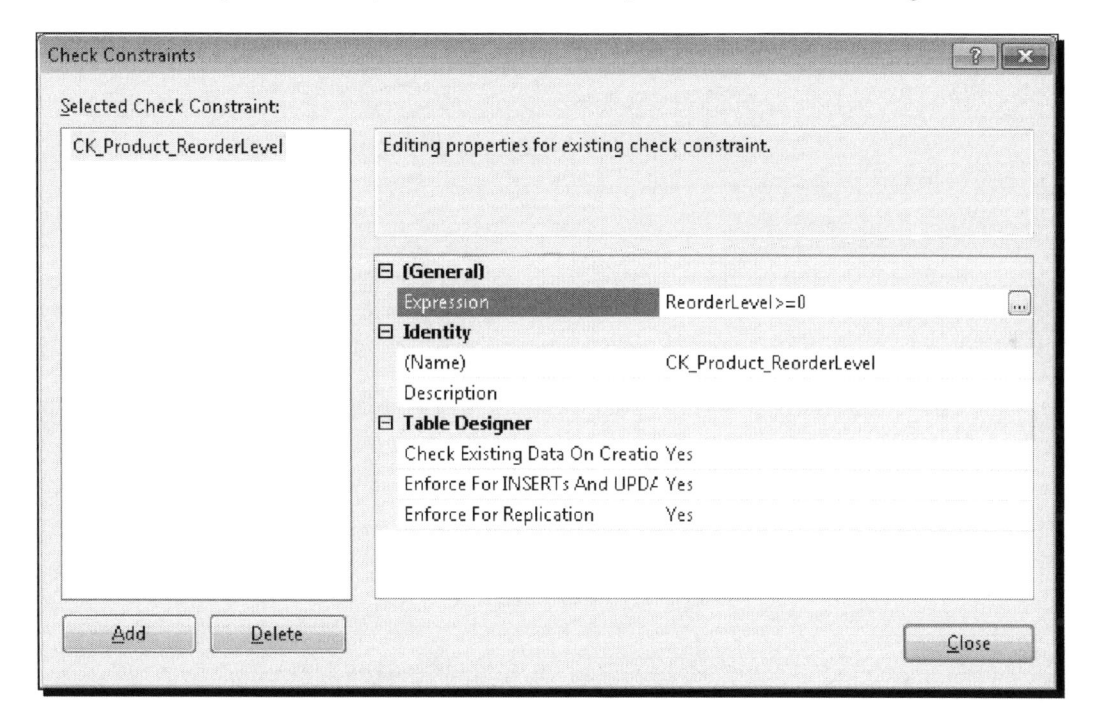

6. Click on **Close** to dismiss the dialog window and return to the table designer.

7. Press *CTRL + S* in the table designer to save the changes.

Defining the Database Schema

8. Verify your changes by right-clicking on the **Constraints** folder of the **Products** table in the **Object Explorer** and selecting **Refresh**. A new child node **CK_Products_ReorderLevel** should appear, as shown in the following screenshot:

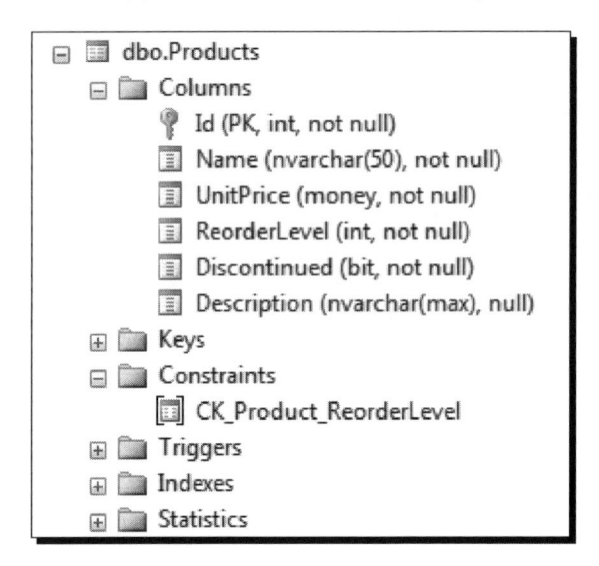

```
□ 🗎 dbo.Products
   □ 🗀 Columns
       🔑 Id (PK, int, not null)
       📄 Name (nvarchar(50), not null)
       📄 UnitPrice (money, not null)
       📄 ReorderLevel (int, not null)
       📄 Discontinued (bit, not null)
       📄 Description (nvarchar(max), null)
   ⊞ 🗀 Keys
   □ 🗀 Constraints
       📄 CK_Product_ReorderLevel
   ⊞ 🗀 Triggers
   ⊞ 🗀 Indexes
   ⊞ 🗀 Statistics
```

What just happened?

In the preceding exercise, we have used SSMS to create a check constraint for a column of the `Products` table. The check constraint assures that we cannot write a negative value into the column `ReorderLevel`.

Time for action – Creating a script to add a check constraint

Now we want to define the script which allows us to add a check constraint to the `Products` table.

1. Open the file `0001_create_Products_table.sql` we created during the preceding exercises.

2. At the very end of the file, add a statement to delete the check constraint to be defined, if it already exists. The code should look similar to the following code snippet:

```sql
IF EXISTS (SELECT * FROM sys.check_constraints
    WHERE object_id = OBJECT_ID('CK_Products_ReorderLevel')
    AND parent_object_id = OBJECT_ID('Products'))
ALTER TABLE Product DROP CONSTRAINT CK_Products_ReorderLevel
GO
```

3. Add code to add a check constraint to the column `ReorderLevel` of the `Products` table which ensures that no value less than zero can be entered. You should come up with something like the following code snippet:

```
ALTER TABLE Products
ADD CONSTRAINT CK_Products_ReorderLevel
CHECK (ReorderLevel>=0)
GO
```

4. Save the file.

What just happened?

Using a simple editor, such as Notepad, we have defined a script which allows us to create a check constraint for the `ReorderLevel` column of the `Products` table. This script can now be used and reused again many many times. While, if we use the designer, we would have to repeat the same steps over and over again.

Indices

A database uses indices to (sometimes) dramatically improve the data access speed. Indices can be created using one or more columns of a database table.

If there was no such thing as indices in a database, and if the database contained a table and this table grows in size over time and might contain millions of records, then the access speed would be extremely disappointing. Why? Well, given a certain query, the database would have to traverse the whole table to locate the requested data. This is also called a **full table scan**. By using indices, the database can optimize the query and avoid traversing the whole table.

When defining an index on a table field or column, the database system creates a structure which contains the values of the sorted indexed field together with the corresponding Primary Key. As the indexed values are sorted, the database can now find the requested values much faster by using a B-tree algorithm. Once the values are located, then the database uses the associated Primary Keys to access the full records in the table.

Defining the Database Schema

Time for action – Adding an index using the designer

In this exercise, we want to add an index to the `Products` table. In our ordering system, we want to have the possibility to search for products by name. To make this search fast, we define an index for the **Name** column.

1. In SSMS, locate the **Products** table in the **Object Explorer**.

2. Right-click on the **Products** table and select **Design**. The designer for the **Products** table will open in a new tab.

3. Right-click on any of the columns in the **Products** designer and select **Indexes/Keys...**, as shown in the following screenshot. The **Indexes/Keys...** dialog window will open.

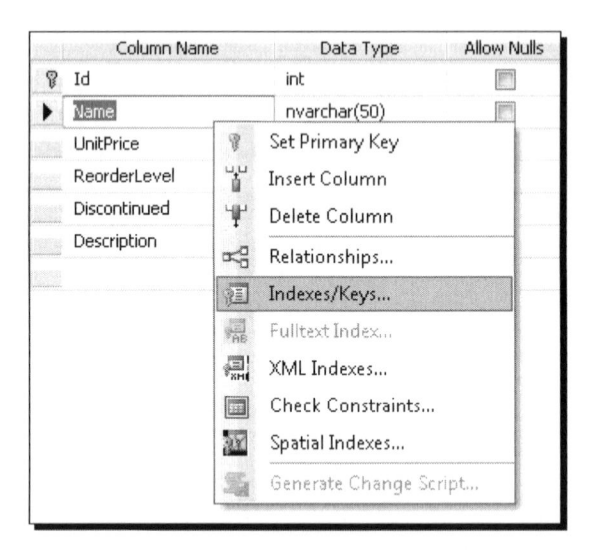

4. Click on **Add** to add a new index and set the properties as follows:
    a. Change the **(Name)** to **IX_Products_Name**.
    b. Choose **Name (ASC)** as the column name to be indexed.
    c. Set **Type** to **Index**.
    d. Set **Is Unique** to **Yes**.

5. Leave all the other settings as the default values, as shown in the following screenshot:

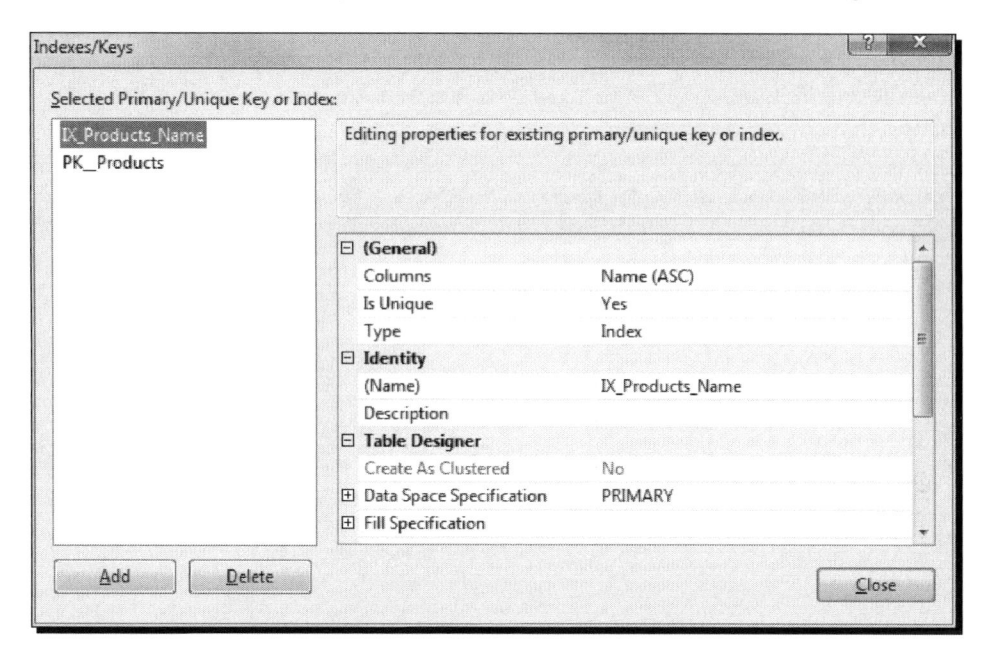

6. Click on **Close** to close the **Indexes/Keys...** dialog window.

7. Back in the **Products** table designer, press *CTRL + S* to save the newly created index.

8. Verify that the index has been created by right-clicking on the **Indexes** node of the **Products** table in the **Object Explorer** and choosing **Refresh**. The new index **IX_Products_Name** should appear as a new child of the **Indexes** folder, as shown in the following screenshot:

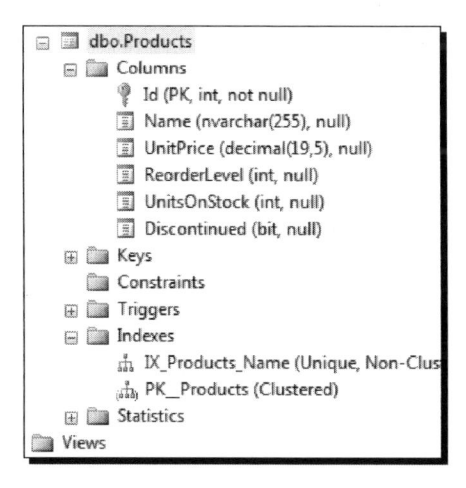

Defining the Database Schema

What just happened?

Using the visual designer of SSMS, we have added an index to the Products table. The index we defined allows us to efficiently query and filter the name of the product records stored in the database table. Our queries will remain efficient, even if the content of the table grows to many millions of entries.

Time for action – Creating a script to add an index

In this exercise, we want to create a SQL DDL script to add the same index to the Products table as defined in the preceding exercise using the SSMS table designer.

1. Open the 0001_create_Products_table.sql file we created during the preceding exercises.

2. At the very end of the file, add a statement to delete the IX_Products_Name index if it already exists. The code is as shown in the following code snippet:

```sql
IF  EXISTS (SELECT * FROM sys.indexes
   WHERE object_id = OBJECT_ID('Product')
   AND name = 'IX_Products_Name')
DROP INDEX IX_Products_Name ON Product
GO
```

3. Add an alternate table statement to add the index to the Products table. Your code should look similar to the following code snippet:

```sql
CREATE UNIQUE INDEX IX_Products_Name
ON Product (Name ASC)
GO
```

4. Save the file.

What just happened?

Once again, we have used a simple editor to define a script which adds an index to the Name column of the Products table. Also pointed out are the advantages of defining scripts over doing the same work by using the various visual designers of SSMS is the repeatability of the work. Scripts can be applied repeatedly without any further work, whereas visual designers always require the work to be redone over and over again.

Normal form

To optimize data storage and retrieval, and to avoid errors introduced by redundant data, relational databases normalize data. The process of organizing data to minimize redundancy is called **normalization**. Edgar F. Codd, the inventor of the relational model, which is the base of relational databases, introduced the concept of normalization. He defined what we now know as the First Normal Form (1NF) in 1970. A year later he introduced and defined the Second and Third Normal Form (2NF and 3NF).

- **1NF**: A table is free of repeating groups.
- **2NF**: Non-key attributes must depend on the whole key.
- **3NF**: Non-key attributes are dependent on "nothing but the key".

To be 1NF compliant, we need to eliminate duplicate columns from the same table, create separate tables for each group of related data, and identify each row with a unique column or set of columns (the Primary Key). In other words, we don't want to store duplicate data, we want to store it once and relate to it.

Essentially, a 3NF database will store data in multiple tables to normalize the data and reduce duplication as we talked about earlier, and additionally:

- Functional dependencies on non-key fields are eliminated by putting them in a separate table. At this level, all non-key fields are dependent on the Primary Key.
- A row is in 3NF if, and only if, it is in 2NF and if attributes that do not contribute to a description of the Primary Key are moved into a separate table.

Putting it all together

Now that we have all the concepts of database tables and relationships sorted out, let's add some tables to our **OrderingSystem** database.

Time for action – Creating a schema for the order entry system

The goal of this exercise is to create a schema that matches the needs of our model to store data. From the preceding exercises, we already have the table `Products` defined in the **OrderingSystem** database. So let's add the remaining tables:

1. Open SSMS and locate the **OrderingSystem** database in the **Object Explorer**. Expand the **OrderingSystem** node such that the **Tables** folder is visible.

2. We want to define the `Employees` table. Right-click on the **Tables** folder and select **New Table…**. A new tab opens with the table designer for the new table.

Defining the Database Schema

3. Add a column `Id` of type `int`. Right-click on the column and select **Set Primary Key** to make it the Primary Key of the table. Note that the **Allow Nulls** is automatically set to false as a Primary Key can never be **null**.

4. Add columns `LastName`, `MiddleName`, and `FirstName`, all of type `nvarchar(50)`. `LastName` and `FirstName` have **Allow Nulls** unchecked, as shown in the following screenshot:

Column Name	Data Type	Allow Nulls
Id	int	☐
LastName	nvarchar(50)	☐
MiddleName	nvarchar(50)	☑
FirstName	nvarchar(50)	☐
		☐

5. Press *CTRL + S* to save the table and when asked, name it `Employees`.

6. Now we define the `Customers` table. Right-click on the **Tables** folder in the **Object Explorer** and select **New Table…**.

7. Add a Primary Key column `Id` of type `int`.

8. Add a column `CustomerIdentifier` of type `nvarchar(50)` and set **Allow Nulls** to false.

9. Add columns `LastName`, `MiddleName`, and `FirstName` all of the type `nvarchar(50)`. Set **Allow Nulls** for `LastName` and `FirstName` to false.

10. Add columns `Line1` and `Line2` of type `nvarchar(100)` and for `Line1` set **Allow Nulls** to false.

11. Add a column `ZipCode` of type `nvarchar(10)` and set **Allow Nulls** to false.

12. Add a column `City` of type `nvarchar(50)` and set **Allow Nulls** to false.

13. Add a column `State` of type `nchar(2)` and set **Allow Nulls** to false.

14. Press *CTRL + S* to save the table and when asked name it `Customers`.

15. Next, we define the `Orders` table. Select **New Table…** to add a new table.

16. Add a Primary Key column `Id` of type `int`.

17. Add a field `CustomerId` of type `int`. Set **Allow Nulls** to false. This is the foreign key to the table `Customers`.

18. Add a field `EmployeeId` of type `int`. Set **Allow Nulls** to false. This is the foreign key to the table `Employees`.

19. Add a field `OrderDate` of type `datetime`. Set **Allow Nulls** to false.

20. Add a field `OrderTotal` of type `money`. Set **Allow Nulls** to false, as shown in the following screenshot:

Column Name	Data Type	Allow Nulls
🔑 Id	int	☐
CustomerId	int	☐
EmployeeId	int	☐
OrderDate	datetime	☐
OrderTotal	money	☐
		☐

21. Press *CTRL + S* to save the table and give it the name `Orders`.

22. Now, select **New Table...** again to define the `LineItems` table.

23. Add a Primary Key column `Id` of type `int`.

24. Add a field `OrderId` of type `int`. Set **Allow Nulls** to false. This is the foreign key to the table `Orders`.

25. Add a field `ProductId` of type `int`. Set **Allow Nulls** to false. This is the foreign key to the table `Products`.

26. Add a field `UnitPrice` of type `money`. Set **Allow Nulls** to false.

27. Add a field `Discount` of type `money`. Set **Allow Nulls** to false.

28. Add a field `Quantity` of type `int`. Set **Allow Nulls** to false.

29. Press *CTRL + S* to save the table and give it the name `LineItems`.

We have defined all tables that make up our ordering system. It is now time to define the relations among those tables.

30. Open the table designer for the `LineItems` table.

31. Right-click inside the designer and select **Relationships...**. The **Foreign Key Relationships** dialog window will open.

32. Click on **Add** to add a new relationship.

Defining the Database Schema

33. Change the **(Name)** to **FK_LineItems_Products** as we want to define a relationship between the `LineItems` and the `Products` table, as shown in the following screenshot:

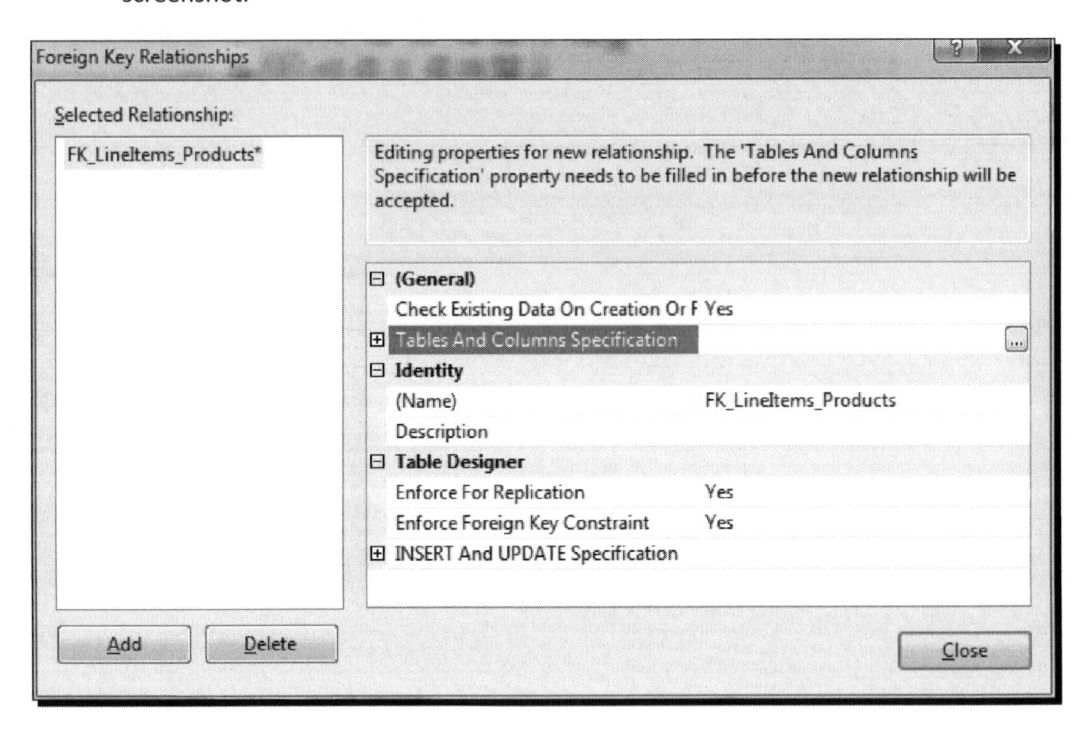

Foreign Key Relationships

Selected Relationship:

FK_LineItems_Products*

Editing properties for new relationship. The 'Tables And Columns Specification' property needs to be filled in before the new relationship will be accepted.

- **(General)**
  - Check Existing Data On Creation Or F — Yes
  - Tables And Columns Specification
- **Identity**
  - (Name) — FK_LineItems_Products
  - Description
- **Table Designer**
  - Enforce For Replication — Yes
  - Enforce Foreign Key Constraint — Yes
  - INSERT And UPDATE Specification

34. Click on the **...** button next to the **Tables and Columns Specification**. The **Tables and Columns** dialog window will open.

35. Select `Products` as **Primary key table** and `Id` as the column in the Primary Key table.

36. Select the column `ProductId` of the table `LineItems` as the foreign key column, as shown in the following screenshot:

37. Click on **OK** to accept the settings. Back in the **Foreign Key Relationships** dialog window, click on **Close** to dismiss the dialog and return to the table designer.

38. In the table designer, press *CTRL + S* to save the changes. A window pops up with a warning that the two tables `Products` and `LineItems` will be saved to the database. Click on **Yes** to confirm and continue, as shown in the following screenshot:

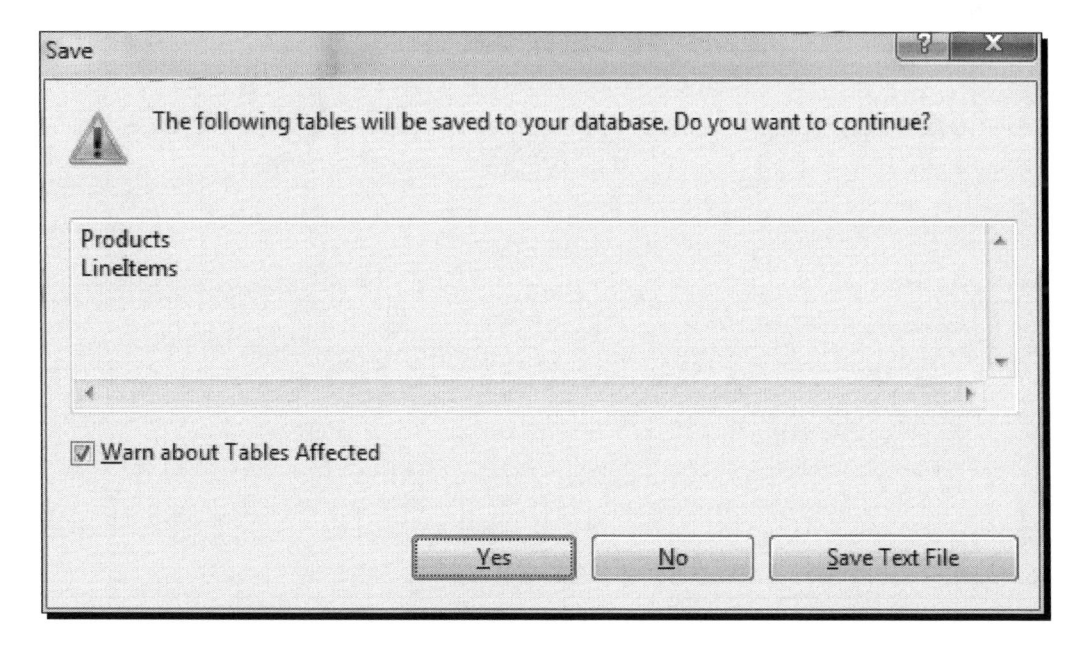

Defining the Database Schema

39. Repeat steps 31 through 38 to add a foreign key relationship between the `LineItems` and the `Orders` tables. Call the relation `FK_LineItems_Orders`. Link the `OrderId` field of the `LineItems` table to the `Id` field of the `Orders` table.

40. Open the table designer for the `Orders` table.

41. Repeat steps 31 through 38 to add a foreign key relationship between the `Orders` and the `Customers` tables. Call the relation `FK_Orders_Customers`. Link the `CustomerId` field of the `Orders` table to the `Id` field of the `Customers` table.

42. Repeat steps 31 through 38 to add a foreign key relationship between the `Orders` and the `Employees` tables. Call the relation `FK_Orders_Employees`. Link the `EmployeeId` field of the `Orders` table to the `Id` field of the `Employees` table.

We have completed the definition of our `OrderingSystem` database. The database schema can be visualized, as shown in the following screenshot:

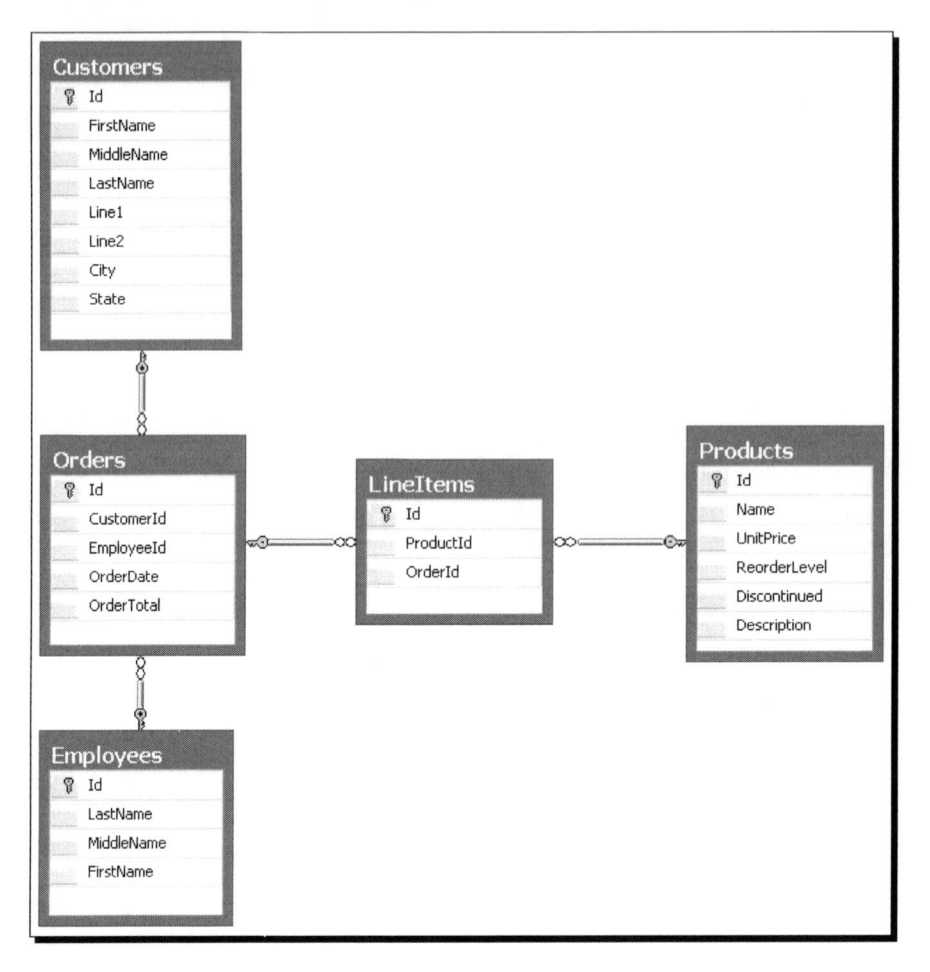

What just happened?

In the preceding exercise, we have used SSMS to create the database schema for our ordering system. We have created all tables as well as their respective Primary Key and the foreign key relationships between the tables.

Have a go hero – Adding an additional table to the schema

Earlier in this chapter, when discussing one-to-one relationships, we mentioned a `ProductPhotos` table. Try to add such a table to the schema and also define the relationship between this new table and the `Products` table.

Have a go hero – Authoring a DDL script to generate the schema

Try to write a script that creates the whole ordering system schema in one go, including all tables, primary key definitions, and foreign key relations.

Do not use database-generated IDs

Most modern database servers, such as MS SQL Server or Oracle, offer the possibility to use database-generated IDs for Primary Keys. In SQL Server, we can auto generate IDs by defining the column to be an identity column. In Oracle, we would use sequences to generate new IDs.

When using NHibernate or any other ORM framework, you will want to avoid this feature of the database as it has many drawbacks.

One of the criteria for a good Primary Key is that it is assigned by an NHibernate Persistent Object ID (POID) generator. Automatic assignment lets NHibernate manage the assignment of Primary Keys. NHibernate has the "smarts" baked right in to create those IDs for us and put them back into our object.

Whenever a record is inserted into the database, it is assigned a number, either the next number in the sequence (that is, high/low), or a randomly assigned GUID (Globally Unique Identifier), depending on which POID you are using.

We will talk more about POID generators and why to use them instead of database-generated IDs in the next chapter.

Views

Views are database objects that are often used to provide read-only access to data stored in the various tables of the database. Views can provide a partial view of a single table or a denormalized view of several joined tables. In this regard, views are very useful for query operations and less useful for data manipulation operations such as creating and updating data. Views can be regarded as virtual tables. No data is stored in a view. Whenever we query a view, the data is retrieved on the fly from the underlying tables.

> Note that MS SQL Server and Oracle allow the definition of materialized views. A materialized view is a database object that contains the result of a query. Or put in other words: the result of the query is precalculated and readily available when needed. In this context, when talking about views, we are not referring to this special type of views.

As an example, let's assume that we want to show in our application a list of the customers with orders that have order totals higher than, let's say, 1000 US$. We can easily get to this data by using a view which combines for us the necessary tables combining the requested values. The following code snippet generates a view which joins tables `Customers` and `Orders`, and filters the data for records whose `OrderTotal` is greater than or equal to 1000 US$. This view can then be used by our application to retrieve the desired data:

```
create view CustomerOrderTotals
as select c.Id,
    c.FirstName,
    c.MiddleName,
    c.LastName,
    o.OrderDate,
    o.OrderTotal
from Customers c
join Orders o on c.Id = o.CustomerId
    where o.OrderTotal >= 1000;
```

What about stored procedures and triggers?

Most modern RDBMSs offer the possibility to define logic inside the database. This can be done in the form of either stored procedures and/or triggers.

A **database trigger** is procedural code that is automatically executed in response to certain events on a particular table or view in a database. Such events can be, for example, the insertion or deletion of a record in a table. The trigger is mostly used to maintain the integrity of the information in the database or to create audit logs.

A **stored procedure** is procedural code that is available to applications accessing the database. The code is stored and executed inside the database. Typical uses for stored procedures include access control, data validation, or data aggregation among many others.

In a modern application that is designed with a model-first approach, the usage of stored procedures (and triggers) is at least controversial. Personally, I tend to avoid triggers completely and stored procedures in most of situations, and only use the latter in very specific scenarios which are difficult or impossible to solve by other means.

Pop quiz

1. Which of the following are elements of a database schema?
    a. Classes
    b. Views
    c. Properties
    d. Events
    e. Stored procedures
    f. Foreign key constraints
    g. Tables

Summary

In this chapter, we have learned what a relational database is and how we can construct such a database which fits our needs to store data generated by our system.

We specifically covered what a database schema is and which elements it comprises. We then learned how we can create database tables to logically partition our data. In addition, we discussed what type of constraints we can use to further structure our data and relate our tables in the schema. Last but not least, we examined the generation of Primary Keys, as well as the usage of triggers and stored procedures in the context of NHibernate.

Now that we have discussed how to model our data into tables, we are ready to bridge the gap between the domain model and the database model or schema. We do this through mapping, which will be discussed in the next chapter.

5
Mapping the Model to the Database

In this chapter, we will discuss the various methods that exist to map a domain model to an underlying database. We will discover that, on one hand, the more we follow conventions, the less we have to code or define, and on the other hand, the more flexibility we want, the more effort we have to invest in the mapping.

In this chapter, we shall:

- Get a clear understanding about what mapping is and what it is needed for
- Discuss in detail four of the most commonly used mapping techniques
- Define and implement conventions to reduce the coding effort
- Automatically create scripts to create a database schema from our mappings
- Define the mapping for our ordering system domain model

Ok then, let's dive into the details.

What is mapping?

In Chapter 3, we introduced the model as one of the core elements of our application. In Chapter 4, we discussed the database schema. Looking back, we realize that there is a huge difference between how the two are defined. The model is object-oriented, whereas the database schema is relational. The former works with individual objects, whereas the latter works with sets of data. There is a conceptual mismatch between the two approaches. We also call this the **impedance mismatch**.

We have to find a means to bridge the gap between the two and that's where mapping comes into play. Mapping defines how the data that lives in the model inside the objects and their properties finds its way into database tables and their fields, defined in a relational database schema. Mapping has a lot to do with wiring up two sides that might look completely different.

When starting a new project from grounds up, a so-called green field project, we want to define the model first and make the database follow out of the model. We do not want to define the database schema first and then try to put our domain model on top of it.

If we make the database schema follow the requirements of the model, then the mapping becomes easy and straight forward. We can use sensible conventions for most parts of the mappings and, as a consequence, we do not have to explicitly define a lot of details. In extreme cases, we can even let the framework automatically create the whole mapping for us.

Types of mapping

When using NHibernate as our ORM framework, we can identify four main types of mappings:

1. XML-based mapping.
2. Attribute-based mapping.
3. Fluent mapping.
4. Convention-based mapping, sometimes also called auto-mapping.

The following section will explain the main concepts behind these different ways of mapping the domain to an underlying database.

> There also exist some OSS and commercial tools that provide the possibility to visually design the mapping between the domain and the underlying database schema. However, this approach is outside the scope of this book.

XML-based mapping

Each type of the model is mapped with an XML document to a table in the database schema. The structure of this XML document is defined in the `nhibernate-mapping.xsd` file, which is part of the NHibernate download.

This way of mapping the model to the database schema is the original and most flexible way to define a mapping. Historically, NHibernate offered only this form of mapping. This flexibility comes at a price. To define an XML document for each and every entity and value object is a lot of work, and XML is not known to be very readable on one hand and very wrist-friendly on the other.

To define a mapping, we add an XML file to the project and give it the extension *.hbm.xml. The XML file has to be an **embedded resource** of the project and its content must follow the structure defined in the .xsd file mentioned above.

> To define an XML file as an embedded resource of the project is the most common way to add a mapping to the application. It is also possible to keep the XML file as an external document. In the latter case, the configuration of NHibernate has to be adjusted accordingly.

When defining the mapping for the Product entity, we would name the mapping file Product.hbm.xml.

To start with the definition of the mapping for the entity Product, we add code similar to the following code snippet to the XML file:

```xml
<?xml version="1.0" encoding="utf-8" ?>
<hibernate-mapping xmlns="urn:nhibernate-mapping-2.2"
  assembly="Sample1"
  namespace="Sample1.Domain">
  <class name="Product">

  </class>
</hibernate-mapping>
```

The preceding XML snippet declares that this shall be a mapping for a class with name Product, which is located in an assembly called Sample1, and the class resides in the namespace Sample1.Domain. The mapping schema definition document used is nhibernate-mapping-2.2.

The various elements in an XML mapping document have to be in a predefined order. The first element we define inside the class node is the mapping of the ID. The following code snippet is used to do this:

```xml
<id name="Id">
   <generator class="native"/>
</id>
```

Here, we have defined that the property Id is to be mapped as the Primary Key and that the Primary Key column's name is also Id. Furthermore, we define that NHibernate shall use the native ID generator to generate the next Primary Key value.

We can then define the mapping for the other properties of the class to be mapped. For example, to map the property Name to the Name field of the database table, we would use the following code snippet:

```
<property name="Name"/>
```

Often people explicitly add the type of the property to the mapping, for example:

```
<property name="Name" type="Int32"/>
```

However, in most cases, this is not needed as NHibernate can automatically determine the right type by using reflection. My recommendation is to not add the type definition to the mapping as this is redundant information and only makes the code noisy. Only add the type definition if it is absolutely needed, as discussed later in this chapter.

On the other hand, we might want to add some constraints to the mapping of the property, such as the definition that the content of the database field cannot be undefined and that the maximum length of the field is 50 characters. We can do so by adding this information via attributes to the corresponding property node:

```
<property name="Name" not-null="true" length="50"/>
```

Putting it all together, the mapping document for the Product class looks similar to the following code snippet:

```
<?xml version="1.0" encoding="utf-8" ?>
<hibernate-mapping xmlns="urn:nhibernate-mapping-2.2"
  assembly="Sample1"
  namespace="Sample1.Domain">
  <class name="Product">
    <id name="Id">
      <generator class="native"/>
    </id>
    <property name="Name" not-null="true" length="50"/>
    <property name="UnitPrice" not-null="true" />
    <property name="ReorderLevel" not-null="true" />
    <property name="Discontinued" not-null="true" />
  </class>
</hibernate-mapping>
```

The most compelling advantage of XML mapping so far is that it is the most complete form of defining mappings. If we can't define a mapping in XML, then we can't define it in any other type of mapping. At the time of writing, some very exotic types of mappings are still only possible in XML.

On the other hand, XML mapping is a very verbose form of mapping and the readability of the mapping documents is limited in comparison with other types of mappings.

Attribute-based mapping

Instead of introducing a separate document to map an entity to an underlying database table, one can also use attributes to decorate the entity and its members. These attributes with their metadata define the details of the mapping. There are several pros and cons regarding this method of mapping the model to the database. The advantages are:

- As already mentioned, we do not have to introduce yet another document to define the mapping.
- Definition of entity and mapping are in one place, therefore it is easier to understand how the entity is mapped.
- The mapping is type-safe and defined in C#. There is no need to use yet another language (such as XML) to define the mappings.

There are also, of course, disadvantages to consider when using this method:

- When adding attributes to our domain entities, we couple the entities tightly to concern to persistence. Our entities are no longer POCO (Plain old CLR objects).
- The introduction of attributes clutters our entities and can makes it harder for the developer to follow what business logic the entity contains.
- Attributes are very limited in their usage. A lot of more advanced mapping scenarios cannot be achieved with attributes, or it is only possible to achieve the desired result in a very convoluted way.

There are two major frameworks available that offer attribute-based mapping. The first one is in an NHibernate contribution project, the second one is part of the larger framework Castle Active Records.

Attribute-based mapping has lost a bit of its appeal with the introduction of fluent or convention-based mapping.

Let's look at a sample. How would we map the `Product` entity when using the NHibernate contribution project?

When mapping an entity, we have to define details on the class itself and on the properties and/or fields of the class. Methods never have to be mapped. On the class level, we define such things as:

- Which table do we want to map the class to; and optionally:

- What is the name of the schema of the table in the database?

```
[Class]
public class Product
{

}
```

The preceding code snippet would map our entity Product to a database table with the same name. If we want to use a different name for the database table, then we can do so by adding this information to the Class attribute:

```
[Class(TableName="Products")]
public class Product
{

}
```

To map a property to a table field, we decorate it with the Property attribute. The following code snippet would map the Name property to the field Name of the table Products:

```
[Class(TableName="Products")]
public class Product
{
  [Property]
  public string Name { get; set; }
}
```

As with the Class attribute, the Property attribute can also be used by specifying more data to refine our mapping of the corresponding property. Such refinements could be the selection of a column name that is different from the property name, or the definition of a maximal length of the database field, or the definition that the field must contain a value that is, it cannot be null, and so on.

```
[Property(Column="ProductName", Length=50, NotNull=true)]
public string Name { get; set; }
```

The preceding code snippet maps the property Name to the table field ProductName, defines the column to be not null, and defines its length to be 50.

Last but not least, let's see how we can define the mapping for the ID of the entity to the Primary Key column of the corresponding table, as shown in the following code snippet:

```
[Id(Column="ProductID")]
[Generator(Class="native")]
public int Id { get; set; }
```

Here, we defined that the property `Id` of the `Product` entity is the ID (also known as Primary Key) of the entity and shall be mapped to the database table field `ProductID`. Furthermore, we define that NHibernate shall use the `native` generator to create new IDs.

In a similar way, we can also define relations and class hierarchies by using attributes, but this exceeds the scope of this book.

Putting it all together, we have the following code snippet:

```
[Class(Name = "Products")]
public class Product
{
   [Id(Column = "ProductID")]
   [Generator(Class = "native")]
   public int Id { get; set; }

   [Property(Column = "ProductName", Length = 50, NotNull = true)]
   public string Name { get; set; }

   [Property(NotNull = true)]
   public decimal UnitPrice { get; set; }

   [Property(NotNull = true)]
   public int ReorderLevel { get; set; }

   [Property(NotNull = true)]
   public bool Discontinued { get; set; }
}
```

Very simple to set up indeed, but, on the other hand, look how noisy our class definition has already got, and this does not include using other attributes for the definition of additional concerns, such as validation or indexing to enable full text search.

Fluent mapping

In this case, the mapping of domain entities to the underlying database tables happens in a type-safe way using a fluent API, which makes the code very readable and concise. The mapping is defined in a separate class and thus does not pollute the entity. The framework, which provides us with the possibility to fluently define the mapping, uses expression trees and static reflection to provide us the type-safety, where we don't have to use "magic strings". The framework Fluent NHibernate (see http://www.fluentnhibernate.org) provides us with the possibility to fluently define our mappings.

Mapping the Model to the Database

Let's look at how we would map the `Product` entity when using fluent mapping. To start with, we add a class to our project that inherits from `ClassMap<T>`, where `T` will be the class we want to map. It makes sense to call all mapping classes the same way as the class we want to map with a postfix `Map`. In our case, the definition would be:

```
public class ProductMap : ClassMap<Product>
{…}
```

In the constructor of the class, we then define the details of the mapping. Basic properties are mapped using the `Map` method of the base class and passing as a parameter, a lambda expression, defining the property of the class we want to map. For the `Name` property of the `Product` class, we would add the following code:

```
public ProductMap()
{
   Map(x =>x.Name);
}
```

The preceding code snippet would map the property `Name` to the field `Name` of the database table `Product`. This is based on the fact that Fluent NHibernate uses sensible conventions if we do not specify things explicitly. If we want to be more specific, then we can do so. To define that the field `Name` cannot be undefined and that its maximum length is 50 characters, we would use the following code:

```
Map(x =>x.Name)
   .Not.Nullable()
   .Length(50);
```

To map the ID of an entity, we use the method `Id` of the base class and again pass a lambda expression, which defines the property which is the `Id` of the entity:

```
Id(x =>x.Id);
```

The preceding code would map the property `Id` as the Primary Key to the field `Id` of the database table `Product`. Furthermore, the native ID generator of NHibernate would be used to generate new Primary Key values.

If we want to be more specific, then we can do so and, for example, map the property `Id` to a database field with a different name, `ProductID`, and define that the `GuidComb` algorithm shall be used for ID generation with the following code:

```
Id(x =>x.Id, "ProductID")
   .GeneratedBy.GuidComb();
```

It is very important that we only define those details that deviate from the defaults determined by the base conventions of the framework. Any unnecessary details are only noise in our code and obfuscate our view to the essential elements.

Putting it all together, we would have the following code to map the `Product` entity to the database table `Product`, having fields with the same names as the properties of the entity:

```
public class ProductMap : ClassMap<Product>
{
  public ProductMap()
  {
    Id(x =>x.Id);
    Map(x =>x.Name).Length(50).Not.Nullable();
    Map(x =>x.UnitPrice).Not.Nullable();
    Map(x =>x.ReorderLevel).Not.Nullable();
    Map(x =>x.Discontinued).Not.Nullable();
  }
}
```

The advantages of mapping fluently are apparent, when looking at the preceding code:

- The code used to define the mapping is very readable and concise.
- The mapping is kept separate from the entity, and thus does not pollute the entity.
- The mapping is type-safe. We use no magic strings.
- Possible selections or settings for each element are very discoverable as the fluent API is fully supported by IntelliSense.

As usual, there is no such thing as a free lunch and we also have to name some disadvantages of the fluent mapping:

- We have to define a mapping class for each entity and value object.
- Some admittedly exotic mapping scenarios are not supported by fluent mapping, though the situation improves with every new release of Fluent NHibernate.
- Currently, defining the mappings fluently introduces a slight performance penalty when starting the application and initializing NHibernate as the fluent mappings have to be translated into XML mappings, which will then be parsed and used by NHibernate. This additional step is not necessary when defining the mappings directly in XML.
- When the name of the database table differs from the entity name or the database field name differs from the property name of the entity, then we have to use magic strings. Unfortunately, there is no way around it.

Mapping by convention

Ideally, we would want the mapping to happen auto-magically. We ask ourselves, "Why can the system not be clever enough to wire itself up?". We are lucky! It is indeed possible to let the system do nearly all of the wiring. How is this possible? The base for this is the definition and usage of sensible conventions. A framework can analyze our domain and use reflection to obtain a lot of metadata about the entities, such as their names and what properties they contain, as well as the type of properties.

We can exchange any of the base conventions with our own implementation, and thus influence in detail how the auto-mapping is executed.

As with the other types of mappings, we want to look at some of the advantages as well as some of the disadvantages of auto-mapping. The most compelling advantages are:

- It requires a lot less code as no explicit mapping between domain and database schema is needed.
- The database schema follows the domain model as close as possible, as the domain model is the main source of metadata from which the database schema is created by the system.
- As developers, we can concentrate on the areas where in our application there are exceptions from the default mapping behavior and address those exceptions explicitly.

And, here are some of the disadvantages:

- As everything is convention-driven, we have much less fine-grained control over the way specific entities are mapped.
- Convention-based mapping is only useful in applications that do not have to deal with already existing legacy databases.

Note that the first of the two "disadvantages" can also be seen as an advantage. It really depends on the context.

A word about lazy loading

In Chapter 3, we defined the domain of our ordering system. Now, we are going to map our domain to an underlying database. Our domain is defined such that it is possible to navigate from one entity to another via the relations we have defined. As an example, we can navigate from our order entity to the line item entities that are associated with the specific order. Furthermore, from a line item we can navigate to the product entity, which this given line item represents inside the order. Theoretically, we can start at one point in the domain and pick one entity, and then navigate throughout the whole domain. As long as we are in the domain and our domain is not connected to any database, this is not a problem, but it can have unwanted side effects as soon as we start to hydrate our domain with data from a database.

Loading data on demand

Which data should NHibernate load for us when we instruct it to load, for example, a customer? Should NHibernate load only the customer data or should it also load all its orders? In addition, if it loads all orders, should it then also load all details of the ordered products? Now, having the products, should it also get the categories the products are associated with? We can continue asking these questions until NHibernate has loaded the whole database.

As we like to have the ability to navigate through the domain via the relations we defined, but, on the other hand, want to avoid that NHibernate loads too much data (in extreme cases, we can cause NHibernate to load the whole database), then we need to introduce a mechanism which allows us to always have just the data loaded we really need. Here comes **lazy loading** to the rescue! NHibernate has, since its very beginning, supported the idea that data is only to be loaded when it is really needed. This behavior is called lazy loading as NHibernate sits around lazy and only does what it is told to do.

Proxies

Now, how can NHibernate make lazy loading happen? NHibernate needs some way to hook into our entities and intercept operations we execute on certain properties of these entities. For this purpose, NHibernate is using proxies. A **proxy** is a class that is "wrapped" around another class and acts on its behalf. When NHibernate loads data from the database and creates an entity, say a product, it does not return an instance of type `product` to us, but rather a proxy to the product. To us, this proxy seems to be a product as it behaves like a product. This is possible due to the fact that the proxy is inherited from the `Product` class and just overrides all its virtual members.

Virtual properties and methods

The preceding section has some important implications. To be able to leverage lazy loading of NHibernate, our domain entities must define all their public properties and their public methods as `virtual`. Only in this case can NHibernate successfully proxy these entities for us.

Creating database schema creation scripts

The nice thing about the model first approach is that we can instruct NHibernate to automatically generate the creation scripts for the database schema for us. That is, we do not have to manually create the database schema, just let NHibernate figure out how the tables and their relations are going to look. To do its job, NHibernate uses the information we provide when defining the mappings for our domain model.

For this job, NHibernate provides us with a class called `SchemaExport`, which expects a `Configuration` object as the parameter of its constructor.

```
var configuration = ...
var exporter = new SchemaExport(configuration);
```

We can then call the `Execute` method, which has several overloads. These overloads can be used to either only create SQL scripts, or to directly create the schema in the database, among other possibilities. Note that there has been no mention of how the configuration object is defined. This will be discussed in detail in Chapter 8, which talks about configuring NHibernate.

To generate the SQL scripts and write them to the console, we can use the following code:

```
var configuration = ...
var sb = new StringBuilder();
var writer = new StringWriter(sb);
var exporter = new SchemaExport(configuration);
exporter.Execute(true, false, false, null, writer);
Console.WriteLine(sb);
```

As an alternative way to produce the same result, we can use the `Create` method of the `SchemaExport` class and provide the action `s=>sb.AppendLine(s)` as the first parameter to the method. The action adds a string `s` to a predefined `StringBuilder` object `sb`:

```
var configuration = ...
var sb = new StringBuilder();
var exporter = new SchemaExport(configuration);
exporter.Create(s =>sb.AppendLine(s), false);
Console.WriteLine(sb);
```

Still, we have not defined where the `configuration` object comes from.

We can use the Loquacious configuration of NHibernate 3 to create such a configuration object for us. In the following code snippet, we have assumed that the mappings have been defined as embedded XML documents and that we are accessing a MS SQL Server 2008 database server:

```
var configuration = new Configuration();
configuration.DataBaseIntegration(db =>
{
  db.Dialect<MsSql2008Dialect>();
  db.Driver<SqlClientDriver>();
});
configuration.AddAssembly(typeof(Product).Assembly);
```

We can also use Fluent NHibernate to create such a configuration object for us:

```
var connString = "server=.\\SQLEXPRESS;database=OrderingSystem;" +
  "integrated security=SSPI;";

var configuration = Fluently.Configure()
  .Database(MsSqlConfiguration.MsSql2008
  .ConnectionString(connString)
  )
  .Mappings(m =>m.FluentMappings
  .AddFromAssemblyOf<Product>())
  .BuildConfiguration();
```

In the preceding case, we assume that we are going to target a MS SQL Server 2008 installed on our local machine having an (empty) database `OrderingSystem` defined. We specify further that when accessing SQL Server, integrated security should be used. Finally, we assume that we have defined our mappings fluently and that all mapping files are defined in the same assembly as the `Product` entity.

Fluent mapping

As already briefly discussed, fluent mapping is a technique where we use a framework that exposes a fluent API to define the mappings for our domain model. The fluent API makes a mapping very readable as there is no unnecessary code noise involved, such as angle brackets.

Fluent mappings are defined in C# and the framework makes heavy use of expression trees to allow us to define all details in a type-safe way without using magic strings. This makes tasks, such as refactoring entities, a breeze as tools such as Visual Studio or ReSharper can automatically refactor the affected mapping files too.

Expression trees – please explain

When Microsoft introduced LINQ for .NET 3.5, it had to first create the necessary infrastructure. LINQ heavily relies on lambda expressions and expression trees. Now, what is an expression tree? Let's try to give a very simple answer: when the compiler parses code, it converts this code into tree-like structures, which can be better analyzed and optimized. Usually, after having created and optimized an expression tree, the compiler compiles it to executable code. However, sometimes it would be nice if developers had the opportunity to work with those trees rather than with the compiled code. Why? It is because an expression tree contains a whole lot of information about the original code and its structure that we can leverage. Analyzing the data stored in the tree and the structure of the tree, we can gain similar and even more information as when using reflection. This analysis of the expression tree is also called static reflection, whereas the standard reflection using the `Type` type of .NET is called dynamic reflection.

Now, let's see how we can use this and show some code. We want to be able to define the mapping for a property of an entity without using magic strings; that is, we want to avoid having code similar to the following line:

```
Map("Some Property");
```

The preceding code snippet uses a string to define which property to map. We'd rather have the following, type-safe code in its place:

```
Map(x => x.SomeProperty);
```

The preceding code uses a lambda expression to define which property we want to map. Note that there are no magic strings involved this time!

Now, the `Map` function is provided by the Fluent NHibernate API and its signature looks similar to the following code snippet:

```
public Property Part<T> Map(Expression<Func<T, object>> expression)
{...}
```

The important part is the type of the parameter `Expression<Func<T,object>>`, which represents an expression tree. In other words, the method `Map` receives an expression tree which it can use to analyze and find out which property we are talking about. Nice!

Getting started

To be able to fluently map our model to the underlying database, we add a reference to Fluent NHibernate and to NHibernate, as shown in the following screenshot. These are, at the moment, the only additional assemblies we have to reference. The two assemblies can be found in the `lib` folder we prepared in *Chapter 2*.

Classes

To map an entity to a database table, we have to add a class to our project that inherits from `ClassMap<T>`, which is defined in the **FluentNHibernate.dll** assembly. This base class contains all the necessary plumbing code that makes the mapping an easy and very straightforward task. To map the `Product` entity, we would start with the following code snippet:

```
public class ProductMap : ClassMap<Product>
{
  public ProductMap()
  {
  // here we define the mapping details
  }
}
```

The mapping has to be defined in the default constructor of the mapping class. Note that `ClassMap<T>` expects the class to be mapped as a generic parameter. In our case, this is the `Product` class.

All details of the mapping have to be defined in the default constructor of the class.

Entity level settings

If we want our database to follow the domain model, then we need to specify the least details. However, for additional flexibility, we have the ability to explicitly specify a lot of details. As an example, we can define the name of the table we want to map the entity to, if it is different from the class name of the entity. We can do so using the following code snippet:

```
Table("tbl_Product");
```

Mapping the Model to the Database

If a specific table resides in another schema than all other tables, then we can also specify the corresponding schema by using the following code snippet:

```
Schema("OrderingSystem");
```

By default, Fluent NHibernate configures our entities to be lazy loaded. If we do not like this, then we can change the behavior by using the following code snippet:

```
Not.LazyLoad();
```

There are many more details we can specify, which are outside the scope of this introduction.

ID columns

The first thing we usually map is the ID of the entity. This is done by using the `Id` method. This method has a lot of options but, in its simplest form, it looks similar to the following code:

```
Id(x =>x.Id)
    .GeneratedBy.HiLo("1000");
```

> Note that the parameter for the `HiLo` method is a string, although internally it is really used as an integer. This is a defect of the current version of Fluent NHibernate.

With the preceding code snippet, we are instructing NHibernate that the property `Id` of the `Product` entity shall be mapped as the Primary Key and that new IDs are to be automatically generated by the `HiLo` generator of NHibernate.

All ID generators defined by NHibernate can be used in the mapping. These are the native generator, the Guid and GuidComb generators, and the `HiLo` generator, as shown previously, among others.

If you want to use GUIDs as your IDs, then you can use the `GuidComb` generator and not the `Guid` generator, as it is optimized for database use. Some sources claim that the performance differences for larger tables can be quite significant when using the `GuidComb` versus `Guid` generator; although this has not yet been proven to be true for all types of database engines and is at least questioned in regards to MS SQL Server 2008.

As long as our field is named `Id` in the database, we are good to go. However, what if it was named `ID` or `PRODUCT_ID`? This simply wouldn't handle it. In that case, we would have to add the optional column parameter to identify it:

```
Id(x =>x.ID, "PRODUCT_ID")
    .GeneratedBy.HiLo("1000");
```

Alternatively, we could write it like the following code snippet:

```
Id(x =>x.ID)
  .Column("PRODUCT_ID")
  .GeneratedBy.HiLo("1000")
```

The former version might be the preferable one, as it is more compact, but on the other hand, you might prefer the latter more explicit version.

An optional attribute that is often used for the ID definition is the `UnsavedValue` function call. This function specifies what value should be returned in a new object before it is persisted (saved) to the database. Adding this call, the code would look similar to the following code snippet:

```
Id(x =>x.ID, "PRODUCT_ID")
  .GeneratedBy.HiLo("1000")
  .UnsavedValue(-1);
```

Note that we did not explicitly define the type of the `ID`. Fluent NHibernate can retrieve this information from the entity by using reflection. In general, we should avoid specifying redundant information as it is not needed and only clutters your code.

Properties

To map simple valued properties, we use the `Map` function. Simple valued properties are properties that have one of the base .NET types, such as `int`, `float`, `double`, `decimal`, `bool`, `string`, or `DateTime`. Such a property is mapped to a single database column. In its simplest form, the mapping of, for example, the `Name` property of the `Product` entity would look similar to the following code snippet:

```
Map(x =>x.Name);
```

The preceding code snippet instructs NHibernate to map the property `Name` to a database column of the same name. The type of the database column would be `nvarchar` in the case of SQL Server and the maximum length of the database column would be 255. Additionally, the column would be nullable.

We can, of course, specify other values if needed. Let's assume that the name column should have a maximum length of 50 and should not be nullable. For this we could use the following code snippet:

```
Map(x =>x.Name)
  .Length(50)
  .Not.Nullable();
```

Mapping the Model to the Database

The beauty of the preceding code snippet is that we can read it as if it were plain English. There are no angle brackets or other noisy code elements that make it hard to read. The fluent API makes things concise and flow nicely.

Assuming that the names of the database columns differ from the property name, we could specify that by using the following code snippet:

```
Map(x =>x.Name, "PRODUCT_NAME")
    .Length(50)
    .Not.Nullable();
```

Sometimes, NHibernate cannot automatically figure out how we want to map a certain property and we have to specify our intent. As an example, we want to map a property which is an `enum` type. Assume the entity `Product` had a property `ProductType` of type `ProductTypes`, where `ProductTypes` is an `enum` like the following code snippet:

```
public enum ProductTypes
{
    ProductTypeA,
    ProductTypeB,
    ...
}
```

Then we can map this property by adding a call to the `CustomType` function, as shown in the following code snippet:

```
Map(x =>x.ProductType)
    .CustomType<ProductTypes>();
```

In this case, as the type behind an `enum` is an integral type (`int` by default), the database field would be of type `int` for an SQL Server. NHibernate will automatically translate between numbers of type `int` in the database and `enum` values in the domain model.

Another example that is often used is the mapping of a property of type `bool` to a `char(1)` database column, which contains 'Y' for `true` or 'N' for `false`. NHibernate has a special mapping defined for this called `YesNo`. We can map, for example, the `Discontinued` property of the `Product` entity as follows:

```
Map(x =>x.Discontinued)
    .CustomType("YesNo");
```

Once again, Fluent NHibernate is very complete and offers us a great deal of flexibility to define the details of mapping a simple valued property. In this section, we have only discussed the most important and frequently used settings. However, let's make one thing clear: in 99% of the cases, this is all you need; but it is good to know that most edge cases are covered by the fluent API.

References

To map a property which references another entity, such as the `Category` property of the `Product` entity, we can map this relation by using code as simple as the following code snippet:

```
References(x =>x.Category);
```

This type of mapping represents a many-to-one relation and is frequently used in a domain model.

Most often, we want to define this reference as a mandatory one. It is very easy and straightforward to do so using the following code snippet:

```
References(x =>x.Category)
   .Not.Null();
```

If we do not specify it explicitly, then the name of the foreign key relating the `Product` table to the `Category` table would be named `Category_Id`. The default convention specifies the foreign key name to be a combination of the name of the Property and ID joined by an underscore character. We can, of course, change this by specifying the name explicitly, as shown in the following code snippet:

```
References(x =>x.Category)
   .Not.Null()
   .ForeignKey("CategoryId");
```

One last noteworthy setting is to specify that a reference shall be unique, as shown in the following code snippet:

```
References(x =>x.Category)
   .Not.Null()
   .Unique();
```

Slowly, you should get a feeling for the concept behind the fluent API.

Collections

Here, we are talking about one-to-many relations. One parent entity holds a collection of child entities. Once again, we can define such a mapping in a very clear and concise way, avoiding any disambiguaties. Let's look at the sample of an order holding a collection of line item objects. The mapping of the line item collection would be similar to the following code snippet:

```
HasMany(x =>x.LineItems);
```

Usually, you want to define your `HasMany` mapping as `Inverse`. What does this mean?

Between the order and a line item, there is an association. We use the inverse attribute to specify the "owner" of the association. The association can have only one owner, so one end has to be set to inverse while the other has to remain "non-inverse".

In this one-to-many association between order and line items, if we don't mark the collection as the inverse end, then NHibernate will perform an additional UPDATE operation. In fact, in this case, NHibernate will first insert the entity that is contained in the collection (the line item), if necessary, insert the entity that owns the collection (the order), and afterwards update the collection entity, so that the foreign key is set and the association is made. Note that in this case, the foreign key in our DB must be nullable.

When we mark the collection end as `Inverse`, then NHibernate will first persist the entity that owns the collection (the order), and will persist the entities that are in the collection afterwards (the line items), avoiding the additional UPDATE statement.

In most cases, the former is not what we want, and thus we add `Inverse` to our mapping, as shown in the following code snippet:

```
HasMany(x =>x.LineItems)
    .Inverse();
```

Another important detail we can configure is the behavior regarding whether and how NHibernate should cascade insert, update, and delete operations from a parent entity to its children. If we specify that NHibernate should cascade operations, then when we add a new line item to the `LineItems` collection of the order, and subsequently save the order, NHibernate will automatically also save this new line item. Without cascading enabled, we would have to explicitly save the line item ourselves. Another important scenario regarding cascading is the case where we remove an existing line item object from the `LineItems` collection of the order. What should happen if we save the order? With the appropriate cascade setting, NHibernate will automatically delete the line item from the database; otherwise we have to do it explicitly.

Most often, you will want to use this setting, as shown in the following code snippet:

```
HasMany(x =>x.LineItems)
    .Inverse()
    .Cascade.DeleteAllOrphans();
```

Mapping many-to-many relations

We can also map the scenario where we have, say, a book that is written by many authors and an author can write many books. In the domain model, the Book entity would have a collection of Author child objects, and at the same time, the Author entity would have a collection of Book child objects. The code to define such a mapping is shown in the following code snippet:

```
HasMany(x =>x.Author);
```

If we want to specify how the intermediate table is called that links the `Author` and `Book` table in this many-to-many relation, then we can do so using the following code snippet:

```
HasMany(x =>x.Author)
   .Table("BookAuthor");
```

Mapping value objects

In Chapter 3, we learned that value objects are a very important concept of a domain model, and thus we need to know how to map a property which has a value object as type. Let's take the `Name` property of the `Customer` entity as an example. First, we might want to map the value object itself. For that, we define a class `NameMap`, which inherits from `ComponentMap<Name>`, as shown in the following code snippet:

```
public class NameMap : ComponentMap<Name>
{...}
```

Then, we add the mapping details to the default constructor of this class, as shown in the following code snippet:

```
public void NameMap()
{
  Map(x =>x.LastName).Not.Null.Length(50);
  Map(x =>x.MiddleName).Length(50);
  Map(x =>x.FirstName).Not.Null.Length(50);
}
```

With the preceding code snippet, we define that `LastName`, `MiddleName`, and `FirstName` are all a maximum of 50 characters long, and that `MiddleName` is an optional value.

Once we have mapped the value object, we can define the mapping for the `Name` property of the `Customer` entity. We add the following code to the default constructor of the `CustomerMap` class:

```
Component(x =>x.Name);
```

Mapping the Model to the Database

Time for action – Mapping our domain

It is now time to define the mapping for our domain model. We want to do this by using fluent mappings as provided by Fluent NHibernate.

1. Start Visual Studio and open the `OrderingSystem` solution from *Chapter 3*.

2. Add references to the assemblies, `FluentNHibernate.dll` and `NHibernate.dll`. To do this, right-click on the **References** node in the **Solution Explorer** window under the **OrderingSystem** project and select **Add Reference...**, as shown in the following screenshot. Navigate to the **lib** folder where all NHibernate and Fluent NHibernate assemblies are located. Select the two files just mentioned.

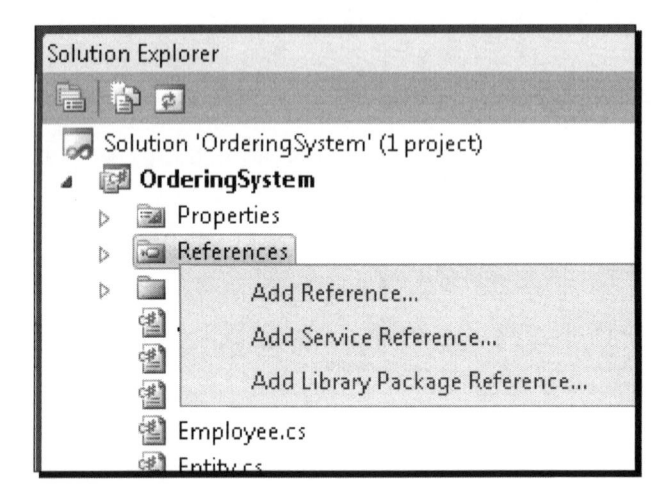

3. In Chapter 3, we used an `ID` of type `GUID` for our entities. In this chapter, we want to use IDs of type `int`. Thus, open the `Entity<T>` class and change the definition of the `ID` property from `public Guid ID{get;set;}` to:

   `public int ID { get; set; }`

4. Also, replace any occurrence of `Guid.Empty` in the code of the `Entity<T>` base class by `0` (zero).

5. In the **Solution Explorer** window, right-click on the **OrderingSystem** project and from the context menu, select **Add | New Folder**, as shown in the following screenshot:

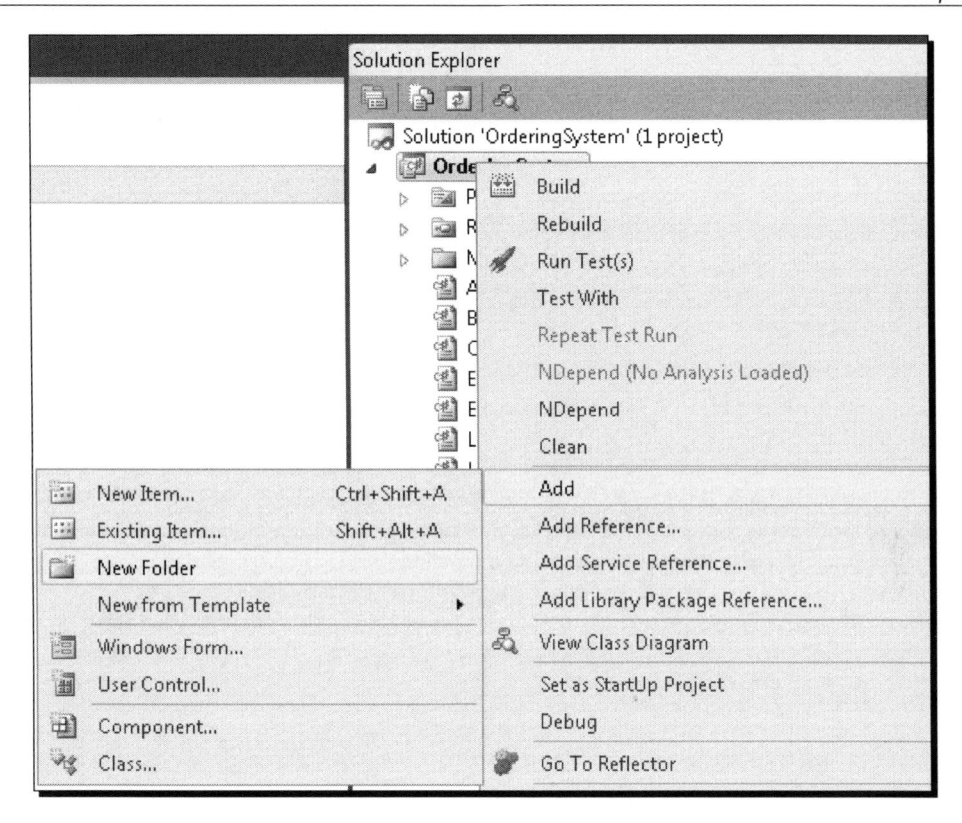

6. Name the new folder **Mappings**. We will put all the mapping classes in this folder.

7. Right-click on the **Mappings** folder and select **Add | New Item…**.

8. In the **Add New Item** dialog, select **Class** from the template list and give it the name `EmployeeMap.cs`. Click on **Add** to add this class to the project and close the dialog.

9. Make the `EmployeeMap` class inherit from `ClassMap<Employee>`. Your code should look similar to the following code snippet:

```
using FluentNHibernate.Mapping;
using OrderingSystem.Domain;

namespace OrderingSystem.Mappings
{
  public class EmployeeMap : ClassMap<Employee>
  {
  }
}
```

Mapping the Model to the Database

10. Add an empty default constructor to the `EmployeeMap` class.

    ```
    public EmployeeMap()
    {
    }
    ```

11. Add code to map the property `ID` of the `Employee` class as Primary Key. We want to use the `HiLo` generator of NHibernate as the generator for (all) our new IDs. We also want NHibernate's `HiLo` generator to work in intervals of 100. To do this, add the following code to the constructor:

    ```
    Id(x =>x.ID)
      .GeneratedBy.HiLo("100");
    ```

    > The HiLo generator used in the preceding code snippet delegates the responsibility to create sequential and unique numbers to be used as IDs for the entities to NHibernate. NHibernate maintains a database table with the current offset for the numbers to generate. We can define an interval (for example, 100 in our sample), during which NHibernate can create subsequent numbers without ever accessing the database. As soon as all numbers of the given interval are used, NHibernate updates the IDs table and takes the next interval of numbers.

12. Add code to the constructor to map the property `Name` of the `Employee` class. As the type of the `Name` property is `Name`, which is a value object, we have a component mapping and the code looks similar to the following code snippet:

    ```
    Component(x =>x.Name);
    ```

13. That is all that is needed to map the `Employee` class. Save the `EmployeeMap` class.

14. Next, we want to map the `Name` value object. Add another class file to the **Mappings** folder of the **OrderingSystem** project (as described in step 7). Name the new class file `NameMap.cs`.

15. Make the class `NameMap` inherit from `ComponentMap<Name>`. Your code should look similar to the following code snippet:

    ```
    using FluentNHibernate.Mapping;
    using OrderingSystem.Domain;

    namespace OrderingSystem.Mappings
    {
      public class NameMap : ComponentMap<Name>
      {
      }
    }
    ```

Chapter 5

16. Add an empty default constructor to the `NameMap` class.

17. Add code to the constructor to map the property `LastName` of the `Name` class. The `LastName` is a mandatory value, and thus cannot be null in the database. Also, the maximum length of the `LastName` shall be 100 characters. This leads to the following code:

    ```
    Map(x =>x.LastName)
      .Not.Nullable()
      .Length(100);
    ```

18. Repeat the preceding step for the `FirstName` property of the `Name` class, as shown in the following code snippet:

    ```
    Map(x =>x.FirstName)
      .Not.Nullable()
      .Length(100);
    ```

19. Map the `MiddleName` property of the `Name` class, as shown in the following code snippet. The middle name is optional, and thus the value can be null in the database. The maximum length is the same as for `FirstName` and `LastName`, as shown in the following code snippet:

    ```
    Map(x =>x.MiddleName)
      .Length(100);
    ```

20. Save the `NameMap` class. With this, the mapping of the `Name` value object is complete and NHibernate knows how to correctly map it when we use it in a `Component` type mapping, as in the `EmployeeMap` class.

21. Now, let's map the `Customer` class. Add a new class file to the **Mappings** folder of the project, as described in step 7, and name the file `CustomerMap.cs`.

22. Make the class `CustomerMap` inherit from `ClassMap<Customer>` and add an empty default constructor to the class, as shown in the following code snippet:

    ```
    using FluentNHibernate.Mapping;
    using OrderingSystem.Domain;

    namespace OrderingSystem.Mappings
    {
      public class CustomerMap : ClassMap<Customer>
      {
        public CustomerMap()
        {
        }
      }
    }
    ```

23. Add code to the constructor to map the property `ID`, as you did for the `Employee` class in step 11.

24. Add code to map the `CustomerName` property of the `Customer` class as a component, as you did for the `Employee` class in step 12.

25. Add code to map the `CustomerIdentifier` property. This property is mandatory and its maximum length should be 50 characters. The last three steps should result in the following code:

```
Id(x =>x.ID)
    .GeneratedBy.HiLo("100");
Component(x =>x.CustomerName);
Map(x =>x.CustomerIdentifier)
    .Not.Nullable()
    .Length(50);
```

26. Add code to map the `Address` property as a component, as shown in the following code snippet:

```
Component(x =>x.Address);
```

27. Now, we need to map the collection of orders of the customer. We want NHibernate to directly access our private field `orders` in the `Customer` class. We also instruct NHibernate to automatically cascade all insert, update, or delete operations from the customer to its orders. The code should look similar to the following code snippet:

```
HasMany(x =>x.Orders)
    .Access.CamelCaseField()
    .Inverse()
    .Cascade.AllDeleteOrphan();
```

28. We have completed the mapping of the `Customer` class. Save the file.

29. Next, we will map the `Address` value object. Add a new class file to the **Mappings** folder of the project, as described in step 7, and name the file `AddressMap.cs`.

30. Make the class `AddressMap` inherit from `ComponentMap<Address>` and add an empty default constructor to the class.

31. Map the properties `Line1`, `Line2`, `ZipCode`, `City`, and `State`. All values are mandatory except `Line2`. The maximum length of all the properties should be 50 except `ZipCode`, which should be a maximum of 10 characters long. The resulting code should look similar to the following code snippet (note: use the same `using` statements as in all other mapping classes):

    ```
    public class AddressMap : ComponentMap<Address>
    {
      public AddressMap()
      {
        Map(x =>x.Line1).Not.Nullable().Length(50);
        Map(x =>x.Line2).Length(50);
        Map(x =>x.ZipCode).Not.Nullable().Length(10);
        Map(x =>x.City).Not.Nullable().Length(50);
        Map(x =>x.State).Not.Nullable().Length(50);
      }
    }
    ```

32. Now, let's map the `Order` class. Add a new class file to the `Mappings` folder of the project, as described in step 7, and name the file `OrderMap.cs`.

33. Make the class `OrderMap` inherit from `ClassMap<Order>` and add an empty default constructor to the class.

34. Add code to the constructor to map the property `Id` as discussed in step 10.

35. Map the two properties `OrderDate` and `OrderTotal`, and make them mandatory (not null), as shown in the following code snippet:

    ```
    Map(x =>x.OrderDate).Not.Nullable();
    Map(x =>x.OrderTotal).Not.Nullable();
    ```

36. Map the `Customer` property as a one-to-many reference and declare it as mandatory, as shown in the following code snippet:

    ```
    References(x =>x.Customer).Not.Nullable();
    ```

37. Finally, map the `OrderLines` property similar to the way we mapped the `Orders` collection of the customer in step 27; as shown in the following code snippet:

    ```
    HasMany(x =>x.LineItems)
      .Access.CamelCaseField()
      .Inverse()
      .Cascade.AllDeleteOrphan();
    ```

38. Next, we come to the `LineItem` entity. Add a new class file, `LineItemMap.cs`, to the project.

Mapping the Model to the Database

39. Make the class inherit form `ClassMap<LineItem>`.

40. Add an empty default constructor.

41. Add code to the constructor to map the property `Id` as discussed in step 11.

42. Map the `Order` and the `Product` properties as a one-to-many references and declare them as mandatory; as shown in the following code snippet:

```
References(x =>x.Order).Not.Nullable();
References(x =>x.Product).Not.Nullable();
```

43. Map the `Quantity`, `UnitPrice`, and `Discount` properties and also declare them as mandatory; as shown in the following code snippet:

```
Map(x =>x.Quantity).Not.Nullable();
Map(x =>x.UnitPrice).Not.Nullable();
Map(x =>x.Discount).Not.Nullable();
```

44. Last but not least, we map the `Product` entity. Add a new class file, `ProductMap.cs`, to the project.

45. Make the class inherit from `ClassMap<Product>`.

46. Add an empty default constructor.

47. Add code to the constructor to map the property `ID` as discussed in step 11.

48. Map the properties `Name`, `Description`, `UnitPrice`, `ReorderLevel`, and `Discontinued`. All except `Description` are mandatory values. The `Name` property should have a maximum length of 50, while the `Description` property has a maximum length of 4,000. This results in the following code snippet:

```
Map(x =>x.Name).Not.Nullable().Length(50);
Map(x =>x.Description).Length(4000);
Map(x =>x.UnitPrice).Not.Nullable();
Map(x =>x.ReorderLevel).Not.Nullable();
Map(x =>x.Discontinued);
```

What just happened?

We defined the mapping for our ordering system domain. By doing this, NHibernate now understands how we want to structure the data from the domain in the database. NHibernate knows which entity is stored in which database table and how the properties are related to the database table fields. It is also clear which foreign key constraints are used at the database level to relate the database tables among each other.

Use mapping conventions

Fluent NHibernate uses a lot of conventions to map our domain model to a database schema. All of these conventions make sense in most of the day-to-day projects. Sometimes, it is important that we are able to add our own conventions to the mapping process, or even replace existing conventions with our own specific implementations. Fluent NHibernate is very flexible in this regard and offers us the possibility to fine-tune the system.

Conventions are added to the system during initialization, that is, before the mappings are processed. In *Chapter 8*, which talks about configuration, we will discuss how to add conventions in detail.

ID conventions

During the definition of the mappings for our ordering system domain, you might have noticed that we had to define the mapping of Id for each entity. Specifically, we had to define that we want to use the HiLo generator for ID generation over and over again. If we did not define the generator to use, then the default convention for ID generation would have been applied. The default convention uses the native generator for ID generation.

We can now override the default convention by implementing our own convention. This is done by implementing the appropriate interface defined by Fluent NHibernate. Each type of convention has its own interface. In the case of the Id convention, we are talking about the interface IIdConvention. The implementation of our own convention is very simple and looks similar to the following code snippet:

```
public class MyIdConvention : IIdConvention
{
  public void Apply(IIdentityInstance instance)
  {
    instance.GeneratedBy.HiLo("100");
  }
}
```

Once this convention is added to the configuration, we can simplify the mapping of Id of all our entities to this:

```
Id(x =>x.Id);
```

Having access to instance of the ID, we can basically manipulate each possible detail. Other meaningful manipulations would be, for example, to define the column name of the Primary Key as being a combination of the entity name and ID. The code for this would look similar to the following code snippet:

```
instance.Column(string.Format("{0}Id", instance.EntityType.Name));
```

Mapping the Model to the Database

Having the preceding convention in place, `Id` of the `Product` class would map to a database field of name `ProductId`, whereas `Id` of `Customer` would map to a database field of name `CustomerId`, and so on.

By now, you certainly get a feeling of the flexibility of the convention-based approach!

Property conventions

We can also easily define conventions for basic property mappings. As an example, let's assume that we want to always map properties of name `Name` to the non-nullable database fields of maximum length 50, regardless of the entity the property is defined in. In this case, we write a class which implements the interface `IPropertyConvention`, as shown in the following code snippet:

```
public class MyNameConvention : IPropertyConvention
{
  public void Apply(IPropertyInstance instance)
  {
    if (instance.Name != "Name") return;
    instance.Length(50);
    instance.Not.Nullable();
  }
}
```

Another useful convention would be to map a property of type `bool` to a `char(1)` field containing `'Y'` or `'N'` for `true` or `false`, respectively. This scenario makes sense when the database is Oracle, which does not natively support a Boolean type for database fields. The code in this case would look similar to the following code snippet:

```
public class MyBoolConvention : IPropertyConvention
{
  public void Apply(IPropertyInstance instance)
  {
    if (instance.Type == typeof(bool))
      instance.CustomType("YesNo");
  }
}
```

This convention is only applied to the mapping of properties that are of type `bool`. If this is the case, then the convention applies the standard custom behavior `"YesNo"` defined by NHibernate to the mapping.

Foreign key conventions

The standard convention for foreign keys names the foreign key database field by taking the name of the entity, which is referenced, and the token ID combined with an underscore. In the case of `Order` referencing `Customer`, the foreign key name in the `Order` table would be `Customer_Id` by convention. If we don't like this and prefer to use a different naming schema, say we want the name in the given sample to be `CustomerId` instead (without underscore), then we can do so by again implementing our own convention. For this scenario, Fluent NHibernate already defines a handy base class from which we can inherit and where we can override the method `GetKeyName`. The code looks similar to the following code snippet:

```
public class MyForeignKeyConvention : ForeignKeyConvention
{
   protected override string GetKeyName(Member property, Type type)
   {
      // property == null for many-to-many, one-to-many, join
      // property != null for many-to-one
      var refName = property == null ? type.Name :property.Name;

      return string.Format("{0}Id", refName);
   }
}
```

With these few examples, we have only scratched the surface of what is possible to influence the behavior of the mapping process. Every single aspect of this process can be fine-tuned by adding yet another convention.

Have a go hero – Implement your own convention

a. Implement a convention that converts the names of properties of an entity to an "Oracle-friendly" format. That is, convert Pascal case names into all uppercase strings with underscores separating the words. For example, convert `LastName` to `LAST_NAME`, or `CustomerId` to `CUSTOMER_ID`. Assign this name as the column name of the respective mapping.
Note that, it is called "Oracle-friendly" as the Oracle database is NOT case sensitive regarding table and field names. Thus, for example, `ProductNumberSuffix` would become `PRODUCTNUMBERSUFFIX`, which is not very readable, and it makes sense to define the field name as `PRODUCT_NUMBER_SUFFIX`.

b. Define a convention which defines all database columns as `not null` by default.

No mapping; is that possible?

When starting a brand new project without any legacy code or database to carry over, it is strongly recommended not to define the mappings all together. We should let the framework do this work for us automatically, based on meaningful assumptions. These assumptions should be applied to the system in the form of conventions and the conventions should be easily modifiable by us. Is this possible? Yes! We even have two possibilities to doing so. The first one is offered by Fluent NHibernate and the second one by ConfORM (see http://code.google.com/p/codeconform).

Auto-mapping with Fluent NHibernate

To be able to do this, first of all you would want to group the entities you want to map in a namespace, which is distinct from the namespace of all other classes defined in the project, which are not entities or value objects. This makes it easier to instruct the AutoMapper about which entities and value objects to include in the mapping. It's suggested that you create a folder Domain in your project to which you move all the entities and value objects.

As we do not explicitly map entities or value objects, we define conventions or exceptions for the AutoMapper. We do this by implementing a configuration class, which inherits from the base class DefaultAutomappingConfiguration provided by Fluent NHibernate. This base class has a lot of virtual methods which can be overridden by us to adjust the system to our needs and help the AutoMapper to do its job.

Assuming that we have moved all our entities and value objects to the same namespace, which contains no other classes than domain classes, we can now define our configuration class, as shown in the following code snippet:

```
public class OrderingSystemConfiguration
  : DefaultAutomappingConfiguration
{
  public override bool ShouldMap(Type type)
  {
    return type.Namespace == typeof(Employee).Namespace;
  }
}
```

The preceding code instructs the AutoMapper to consider only those classes for mapping which reside in the same namespace as the Employee entity.

We need to instruct the AutoMapper about one more thing before it can do its work. We have to instruct it as to which are the value objects in our system. We can do this by overriding the `IsComponent` method in the configuration class, as shown in the following code snippet:

```
public override boolIsComponent(Type type)
{
   var componentTypes = new[] {typeof (Name), typeof (Address)};
   return componentTypes.Contains(type);
}
```

Having this configuration class in place, the AutoMapper is ready to go. If we want to influence more details of the mapping process, like the selection of the ID generator, then we can do so by defining conventions in exactly the same way as we did in the preceding section about fluent mapping.

To configure our system to use auto-mapping, we would use the following code snippet:

```
var cfg = new OrderingSystemConfiguration();
var configuration = Fluently.Configure()
  .Database(/* database config */)
  .Mappings(m =>m.AutoMappings.Add(
  AutoMap.AssemblyOf<Employee>(cfg))
  .BuildConfiguration();
```

Note that the details of the preceding code snippets are not important at this moment and will be explained in detail in Chapter 8, where we will talk extensively about configuring our system.

Time for action – Using auto-mapping

In this sample, we want to define a very basic domain model, map the model using auto-mapping as provided by Fluent NHibernate, and then let NHibernate generate the schema for us, based on this mapping:

1. Start Visual Studio and create a new project. Choose **Console Application** as the project template. Name the project **AutoMappingSample**.

2. Add references to the two assemblies `NHibernate.dll` and `FluentNHibernate.dll` to the project.

3. Add a folder `Domain` to the project.

4. Add a class `Customer` to the `Domain` folder of the project. The customer entity should have `Id` and `CustomerName` as properties, as shown in the following code snippet:

```
public class Customer
{
    public virtual int Id { get; set; }
    public virtual string CustomerName { get; set; }
}
```

5. Add a class `LineItem` to the `Domain` folder of the project. The order line entity should have the properties `Id`, `Quantity`, `UnitPrice`, and `ProductCode`, as shown in the following code snippet:

```
public class LineItem
{
    public virtual int Id { get; set; }
    public virtual int Quantity { get; set; }
    public virtual decimal UnitPrice { get; set; }
    public virtual string ProductCode { get; set; }
}
```

6. Add a class `Order` to the `Domain` folder of the project. The order entity should have an `Id`, an order date, a reference to a customer entity, and a collection of `LineItem` entities, as shown in the following code snippet:

```
public class Order
{
    public virtual int Id { get; set; }
    public virtual DateTime OrderDate { get; set; }
    public virtual Customer Customer { get; set; }
    public virtual IList<LineItem> LineItems { get; set; }
}
```

7. Add a class `OrderingSystemConfiguration` to the project.

8. Make the class inherit from `DefaultAutomappingConfiguration`.

9. Override the method `ShouldMap` of the base class and define which types of the project should be mapped. Be sure to override the right method as there are two overloads of `ShouldMap`; use the one with the parameter type of `Type`, as shown in the following code snippet:

```
public class OrderingSystemConfiguration
    : DefaultAutomappingConfiguration
{
    public override bool ShouldMap(Type type)
```

```
    {
        return type.Namespace == typeof (Customer).Namespace;
    }
}
```

10. Add the following `using` statements to the `Program` class:
    ```
    using System;
    using AutoMappingSample.Domain;
    using FluentNHibernate.Automapping;
    using FluentNHibernate.Cfg;
    using FluentNHibernate.Cfg.Db;
    using NHibernate.Tool.hbm2ddl;
    ```

11. Add code to the method `Main` of the `Program` class to create a NHibernate configuration. The configuration object is created with the configuration API of Fluent NHibernate and shall use auto-mapping. The scripts shall be created for MS SQL Server 2008, as shown in the following code snippet:
    ```
    var cfg = new OrderingSystemConfiguration();
    var configuration = Fluently.Configure()
      .Database(MsSqlConfiguration.MsSql2008)
      .Mappings(m =>m.AutoMappings.Add(
      AutoMap.AssemblyOf<Customer>(cfg)))
      .BuildConfiguration();
    ```

12. Note that it is not necessary to define a connection string for this operation as we are not going to access the database, but just to instruct NHibernate which type of database we want to target.

13. Add code to create and show the SQL scripts on the console, as shown in the following code snippet:
    ```
    var exporter = new SchemaExport(configuration);
    exporter.Execute(true, false, false);
    ```

14. Add the following code snippet to avoid the program from exiting without waiting for a confirmation:
    ```
    Console.Write("Hit enter to exit:");
    Console.ReadLine();
    ```

Mapping the Model to the Database

15. Run the application. The output on the console should look like the following screenshot:

```
create table [Customer] (
    Id INT IDENTITY NOT NULL,
    CustomerName NVARCHAR(255) null,
    primary key (Id)
)

create table [LineItem] (
    Id INT IDENTITY NOT NULL,
    Quantity INT null,
    UnitPrice DECIMAL(19,5) null,
    ProductCode NVARCHAR(255) null,
    Order_id INT null,
    primary key (Id)
)

create table [Order] (
    Id INT IDENTITY NOT NULL,
    OrderDate DATETIME null,
    Customer_id INT null,
    primary key (Id)
)

alter table [LineItem]
    add constraint FKDDD0206A86F33B9D
    foreign key (Order_id)
    references [Order]

alter table [Order]
    add constraint FK3117099BB2299B69
    foreign key (Customer_id)
    references [Customer]
```

16. Note that for brevity, the drop statements of the SQL script have been omitted.

What just happened?

We defined a domain model, created a NHibernate configuration object using auto-mapping, and then used the schema export class of NHibernate to create the database schema, which follows our domain model definition. We didn't have to write any code to define a mapping. Fluent NHibernate automatically generated an implicit mapping for us based on some meaningful default conventions.

If we are not happy with the result, we can fine-tune any aspect of it by defining our own conventions.

Using ConfORM

ConfORM is part of the NHibernate contributions and can be downloaded from `http://code.google.com/p/codeconform`. Make sure you download the version that is compatible with the version of NHibernate you are using. The only additional assembly you need when working with ConfORM is `ConfORM.dll`.

> To select from and use several sets of predefined conventions, you might want to reference the assembly `ConfORM.Shop.dll`. It is worth having a look at the source code for any further details.

Similar to the AutoMapper of Fluent NHibernate, ConfORM uses conventions to implicitly define a mapping for the domain model. These conventions can be overridden by us or we can define our own conventions.

Time for action – Using ConfORM to map our domain

In this example, again we want to create a simple domain model and use ConfORM to create an implicit mapping for us. We then want to use the NHibernate schema exporter to create the SQL script to create a database schema compatible with our domain.

1. Start Visual Studio and create a new project. Choose **Console Application** as the project template. Name the project **ConfORMSample**.

2. Add references to the two assemblies `NHibernate.dll` and `ConfORM.dll` to the project.

3. Create a folder `Domain` in the project.

4. Add classes `Customer`, `Order`, and `LineItem` to the `Domain` folder of the project. The classes should contain the same code as defined in the preceding exercise in steps 4 through 6.

5. To the `Program` class, add the following `using` statements:

   ```
   using System;
   using System.Linq;
   using ConfORMSample.Domain;
   using ConfOrm;
   using ConfOrm.NH;
   using NHibernate.Cfg;
   using NHibernate.Cfg.Loquacious;
   using NHibernate.Dialect;
   using NHibernate.Driver;
   using NHibernate.Tool.hbm2ddl;
   ```

Mapping the Model to the Database

6. In the `Main` method of the `Program` class, add code to create a NHibernate configuration object using the fluent configuration API provided by NHibernate:

   ```
   var configuration = new Configuration();
   configuration.DataBaseIntegration(db =>
   {
     db.Dialect<MsSql2008Dialect>();
     db.Driver<SqlClientDriver>();
   });
   ```

7. Note that for this exercise, we only need to specify the database type we want to create a schema creation script for.

8. Add code to determine the types that need to be mapped, as shown in the following code snippet:

   ```
   var types = typeof (Customer).Assembly.GetTypes()
     .Where(t =>t.Namespace == typeof (Customer).Namespace);
   ```

9. Create an instance of type `ObjectRelationalMapper`, which is defined in the `ConfORM` assembly, as shown in the following code snippet:

   ```
   var orm = new ObjectRelationalMapper();
   ```

10. Instruct this mapper that it should create a table for each type to be mapped, as shown in the following code snippet:

    ```
    orm.TablePerClass(types);
    ```

11. Add code to create the mappings and add them to the configuration object, as shown in the following code snippet:

    ```
    var mapper = new Mapper(orm);
    var hbmMappings = mapper.CompileMappingFor(types);
    configuration.AddDeserializedMapping(hbmMappings, "MyDomain");
    ```

12. Add code to create the schema generation script, as shown in the following code snippet:

    ```
    var exporter = new SchemaExport(configuration);
    exporter.Execute(true, false, false);
    ```

13. Add the following code snippet to avoid the program from exiting without waiting for confirmation:

    ```
    Console.Write("Hit enter to exit:");
    Console.ReadLine();
    ```

14. Run the application and analyze the output. The output should look similar to the following screenshot:

```
create table Order (
    Id INT not null,
    OrderDate DATETIME null,
    Customer INT null,
    primary key (Id)
)

create table LineItem (
    Id INT not null,
    Quantity INT null,
    UnitPrice DECIMAL(19,5) null,
    ProductCode NVARCHAR(255) null,
    order_key INT null,
    idx INT null,
    primary key (Id)
)

create table Customer (
    Id INT not null,
    CustomerName NVARCHAR(255) null,
    primary key (Id)
)

alter table Order
    add constraint FK3117099B351D757
    foreign key (Customer)
    references Customer

alter table LineItem
    add constraint FKDDD0206AD7CB8FD5
    foreign key (order_key)
    references Order

create table hibernate_unique_key (
    next_hi INT
)

insert into hibernate_unique_key values ( 1 )
Hit enter to exit:
```

What just happened?

With no coding and very little configuration effort, we have been able to make the system create an implicit mapping of our domain model for us and export it as a script, which we can then use to generate our database schema.

The script that we generated is based on meaningful conventions defined in ConfORM. All of these conventions can be overridden by us and we can add our own conventions to fine-tune the result to our specific needs.

Mapping the Model to the Database

XML mapping

To add IntelliSense capabilities to Visual Studio for the NHibernate mapping files, we add the .xsd files, which are part of the NHibernate download, to the solution. For this, create a solution folder named **Schema** and add the two XML schema definition files nhibernate-configuration.xsd and nhibernate-mapping.xsd to this folder, as shown in the following screenshot:

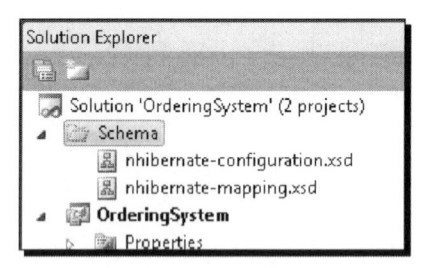

When defining mapping for an entity, we add a new XML file to the project. The file has to have the extension .hbm.xml. As the name of the file, it is recommended to use the name of the entity you want to map, for example, Product.hbm.xml when mapping the Product entity. As shown in the following screenshot:

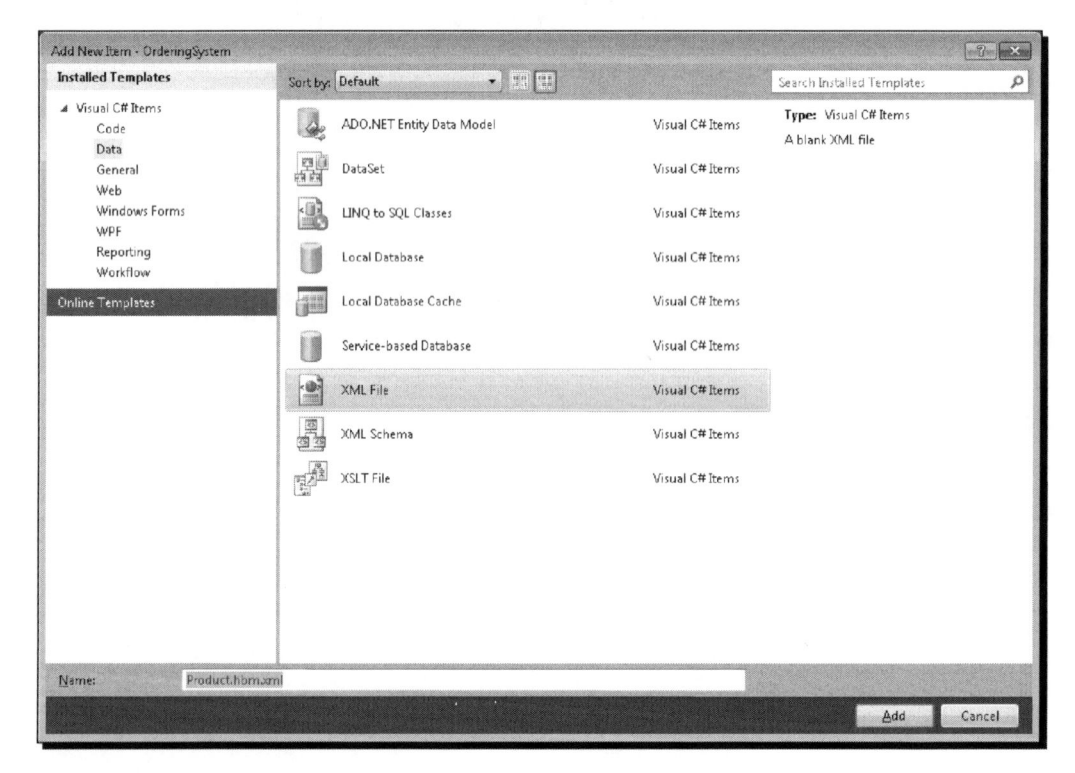

We also set the **Build Action** property of the XML file to **Embedded Resource**, as shown in the following screenshot:

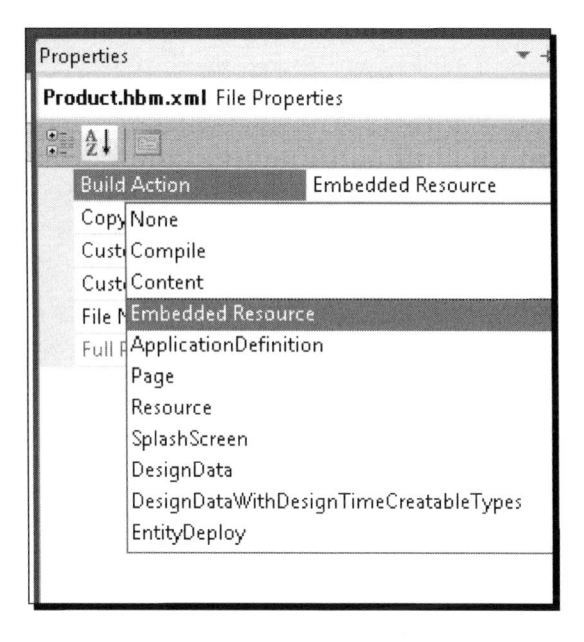

Getting started

The XML mapping document begins like any XML document, with an XML declaration. No magic here, just a simple xml tag and two attributes, version and encoding.

```
<?xml version="1.0" encoding="utf-8" ?>
```

The next tag we are going to see in our document is the hibernate-mapping tag. This tag has an attribute named xmlns, which is the XML namespace that the NHibernate mapping file should be validated against. This is directly related to a version of NHibernate, as each version has its own XML namespace to cover changes in the mapping language.

We can also use this tag to define the namespace and assembly that the class we are mapping resides in. The opening and closing tags for the hibernate-mapping tag are as shown in the following code snippet:

```
<?xml version="1.0" encoding="utf-8" ?>
<hibernate-mapping xmlns="urn:nhibernate-mapping-2.2"
  namespace="OrderingSystem.Domain"
  assembly="OrderingSystem">
</hibernate-mapping>
```

These three properties within the hibernate-mapping tag make up the basic XML mapping document.

Mapping the Model to the Database

Classes

The next tag we need to define in our document is the `class` tag. This is a key tag, because it tells NHibernate two things—the class this mapping document is meant to represent and the table in the database that the class should map to.

The `class` tag has two attributes we need to be concerned with—`name` and `table`.

```
<class name="" table="">
</class>
```

The `name` attribute contains the fully-qualified POCO class that we want to map to, including the assembly name.

> While this can be specified in the standard fully-qualified dotted class name, a comma and then the assembly name, the preferred method is to define the namespace and assembly in the `<hibernate-mapping>` tag, as shown in the code in the previous section.

The `table` attribute specifies the table in the database that this mapping file represents. It can be as simple as the name of the table, `Product`, or as complex as needed, to adequately describe the table.

If you need to include the owner of the table, such as `dbo.Product`, then you can add the `schema` attribute as follows:

```
schema="dbo"
```

If we were going to map the `Product` class in our application to the `Product` table in the database, then we would use a tag as shown in the following code snippet:

```
<class name="Product" table="Product">
</class>
```

> As in this example, the table name is the same as our class name; we should leave out the table attribute to not unnecessarily clutter our code.

Properties

We can map properties from our class to fields in the database using the `id` tag and the `property` tag. These tags are for the standard fields in the database, not the foreign key fields. We'll get to those in a minute.

The `id` and `property` tags follow a standard pattern and have a number of optional parameters. They follow the basic format of defining the property on the class that they are mapping to and the data type that is used to represent that data. This will generally look similar to the following code snippet:

```xml
<property name="Name" type="String">
  <column name="Name" length="255" sql-type="varchar"
    not-null="true"/>
</property>
```

This is the fully verbose method of mapping the properties. Alternately, you can map the property as follows:

```xml
<property name="Name" />
```

Both methods will provide the same mapping to NHibernate but, as stated earlier, the more verbose method gives you a lot of flexibility, while the latter method keeps your code clean and terse, free from unnecessary clutter.

Generally, it is recommended to use the latter method and add more details only if needed.

One of the optional attributes that people often use on the `id` and `property` tags is the `type` attribute. With this attribute, we can instruct NHibernate that we are using a particular data type to store that information in our class. Adding this data type, our `property` tag would look as shown in the following code snippet:

```xml
<property name="Name" type="String" />
```

Again, it is recommended not to use this attribute if NHibernate can determine the property type by reflection. It is only used in scenarios where reflection does lead to an undesired result as, for example, when mapping `string` type properties to a database field of type `CLOB`.

ID columns

The first property from our class that we want to map is the `Id` property. This tag has a number of attributes we can optionally set, but the simplest way we can map the `Id` property is as shown in the following code snippet:

```xml
<id name="Id">
  <generator class="hilo"/>
</id>
```

This instructs NHibernate that we have a property in our class named `Id`, which maps to a field in the database called `Id`, and also that we use the `hilo` generator provided by NHibernate to automatically generate a value for this field. Simple enough!

An optional attribute that is sometimes used on the `id` tag is the `unsaved-value` attribute. This attribute specifies what value should be returned in a new object before it is persisted to the database. By adding this attribute, as well as the `type` attribute we talked about, the code would look similar to the following code snippet:

```
<id name="Id" type="Int32" unsaved-value="null">
  <generator class="hilo"/>
</id>
```

As long as our field is named `Id` in the database, we are good to go. However, what if it was named `id` or `product_id`? This simply wouldn't handle it. In that case, we would have to add the optional column tag to identify it, as shown in the following code snippet:

```
<id name="Id">
  <column name="product_id"/>
  <generator class="hilo"/>
</id>
```

Now we have mapped our `product_id` field from the database into a more standard `Id` property on our class. Some of the additional attributes that are commonly used on the `column` tag are as follows:

- `name`: Defines the name of the column in the database.
- `length`: The length of the field, as defined in the database.
- `sql-type`: The database definition of the column type.
- `not-null`: Whether or not the database column allows nulls. `not-null="true"` specifies a required field.

Again, these optional attributes simply allow you to further define how your database is created. Some people don't even define the database. They just define the `hbm.xml` files and, for example, use `NHibernate.Tool.hbm2ddl` to create a SQL script to do this work!

One-to-many relations

In our domain model, we have the `Order` entity that has a property `LineItems`, which is a collection of `LineItem` entities. Each `LineItem` entity, in turn, has a property `Order` that references the order to which the line item belongs. Let's first look at how we would map the "one" side of the relation, namely the `Order` property in the `LineItem` entity:

```
<many-to-one name="Order" class="Order"
  column="OrderId" not-null="true"/>
```

Here, the `name` attribute defines the name of the property in the `LineItem` class. The `class` attribute defines which class the property references. The `column` attribute instructs NHibernate how the database field is called, which contains the foreign key to the `Order` table. Finally, the `not-null` attribute defines that the `OrderId` foreign key cannot be null.

Now that we have the "one" side mapped, we need to map the "many" side. In the `Order` mapping file, we need to create a `bag` element to hold all of these line items. A `bag` is the NHibernate way of saying that it is an unordered collection allowing duplicated items. We have a `name` element to reference the `class` property, just like all of our other mapping elements, and a `key` child element to instruct NHibernate which database column this field is meant to represent.

```
<bag name="LineItems" inverse="true" cascade="all-delete-orphan">
  <key column="OrderId"/>
  <one-to-many class="LineItem"/>
</bag>
```

If you look at the preceding XML code, then you will see that the `one-to-many` tag looks very similar to the `many-to-one` tag we just created for the other side. That's because this is the inverse side of the relationship. We even tell NHibernate that the inverse relationship exists by using the `inverse` attribute on the `bag` element. The `class` attribute on this tag is just the name of the class that represents the other side of the relationship.

The `cascade` attribute instructs NHibernate how to handle objects when we delete them. Another attribute we can add to the `bag` tag is the `lazy` attribute. This instructs NHibernate to use lazy loading, which means that the record won't be pulled from the database or loaded into memory until you actually use it. This is a huge performance gain because you only get data when you need it, without having to do anything. When we say "get `Order` record with `Id` 14", NHibernate will get the `Order` record, but it won't retrieve the associated line items (`LineItem` records) until we reference `Order.LineItems` to display or act on those objects in our code. By default, lazy loading is turned on, so we only need to specify this tag if we want to turn lazy loading off by using `lazy="false"`.

Many-to-many relations

The other relationship that is used quite often is the many-to-many (MTM) relationship. In the following screenshot, the `BookAuthor` table is used to join the `Book` and `Author` tables. NHibernate is smart enough to manage these MTM relationships for us, and we can "optimize out" the join table from our classes and let NHibernate take care of it.

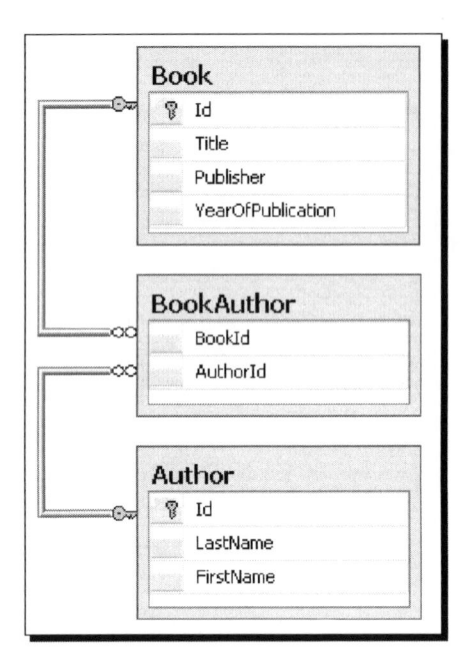

Just like the one-to-many (OTM) relationship, we represent the `Authors` on the `Book` class with a collection of `Author` objects as follows:

```
public IEnumerable<Author> Authors { get; set; }
```

Furthermore, we represent the `Books` on the `Author` class with a collection of `Book` objects, as shown in the following code snippet:

```
public IEnumerable<Book> Books { get; set; }
```

Mapping the MTM is very similar to the OTM, just a little more complex. We still use a `bag` and we still have a `key`. We need to add the `table` attribute to the `bag` element to let NHibernate know which table we are really storing the relationship data in. Instead of a `one-to-many` and a `many-to-one` attribute, both sides use a `many-to-many` element. (Makes sense, it is an MTM relationship, right?). The `many-to-many` element structure is the same as the `one-to-many` element, with a `class` attribute and a `column` attribute to describe the relationship, as shown in the following code snippet:

```xml
<bag name="Authors" table="BookAuthor">
  <key column="BookId"/>
  <many-to-many class="Author" column="AuthorId" />
</bag>
```

From the `Author` side, it looks remarkably similar, as it's just the opposite view of the same relationship, as shown in the following code snippet:

```xml
<bag name="Books" table="BookAuthor">
  <key column="AuthorId"/>
  <many-to-many class="Book" column="BookId" />
</bag>
```

Mapping value objects

To map properties whose type is a value object, we can use the `component` tag. As an example, we see how we would map the property `Name` of the `Customer` entity, as shown in the following code snippet:

```xml
<component name="Name" class="Name">
  <property name="LastName" length="50" not-null="true"/>
  <property name="FirstName" length="50" not-null="true"/>
  <property name="MiddleName" length="50"/>
</component>
```

Time for action – Mapping a simple domain using XML

In this example, we want to create a very simple domain model and map it using XML files. We will then let NHibernate create a SQL schema generation script based on these mapping files.

1. Start Visual Studio and create a new project. Choose **Console Application** as the project template. Name the project **XmlMappingSample**.
2. Add references to the assembly `NHibernate.dll` to the project.
3. Add a new folder to the solution. Call the folder `Schema`.

Mapping the Model to the Database

4. Add the file `nhibernate-mapping.xsd`, which is located in the `lib` folder, to the `Schema` folder. (If the said file is not yet located in your `lib` folder, then please extract it from the ZIP file containing the NHibernate binaries—that you downloaded in Chapter 2—and copy it to the `lib` folder.)

5. Create a folder `Domain` in the project.

6. Add classes `Customer`, `Order`, and `LineItem` to the `Domain` folder of the project. The classes should contain the same code as defined in the exercise at the end of the section about auto-mapping (steps 4 through 6).

7. Add an XML file to the folder `Domain` of the project and call the file `Customer.hbm.xml`. Make sure the **Build Action** of the file is set to **Embedded Resource**.

8. Add the `hibernate-mapping` tag to the file and specify `urn:nhibernate-mapping-2.2` as the value for the `xmlns` attribute. Also, specify the `assembly` and the `namespace` attributes using the correct values, as shown in the following code snippet:

```xml
<?xml version="1.0" encoding="utf-8" ?>
<hibernate-mapping xmlns="urn:nhibernate-mapping-2.2"
    assembly="XmlMappingSample"
    namespace="XmlMappingSample.Domain">
</hibernate-mapping>
```

9. Add code to map the `Customer` entity. Use the `hilo` generator to generate new IDs, as shown in the following code snippet:

```xml
<class name="Customer">
   <id name="Id">
      <generator class="hilo"/>
   </id>
   <property name="CustomerName"/>
</class>
```

10. Add an XML file to the folder `Domain` of the project and call the file `LineItem.hbm.xml`. Do not forget to set the **Build Action** to **Embedded Resource**.

11. Add the following XML to map the `LineItem` entity, as shown in the following code snippet:

```xml
<?xml version="1.0" encoding="utf-8" ?>
<hibernate-mapping xmlns="urn:nhibernate-mapping-2.2"
    assembly="XmlMappingSample"
    namespace="XmlMappingSample.Domain">
   <class name="LineItem">
      <id name="Id">
         <generator class="hilo"/>
      </id>
```

```xml
    <property name="Quantity"/>
    <property name="UnitPrice"/>
    <property name="ProductCode"/>
  </class>
</hibernate-mapping>
```

12. Add an XML file to the folder `Domain` of the project and call the file `Order.hbm.xml`. Set **Build Action** to **Embedded Resource**.

13. Add the following XML to map the `Order` entity, as shown in the following code snippet:

```xml
<?xml version="1.0" encoding="utf-8" ?>
<hibernate-mapping xmlns="urn:nhibernate-mapping-2.2"
  assembly="XmlMappingSample"
  namespace="XmlMappingSample.Domain">
  <class name="Order">
    <id name="Id">
      <generator class="hilo"/>
    </id>
    <property name="OrderDate"/>
    <many-to-one name="Customer" column="CustomerId"/>
    <bag name="LineItems" inverse="true" >
      <key column="OrderId"/>
      <one-to-many class="LineItem"/>
    </bag>
  </class>
</hibernate-mapping>
```

14. Add the following `using` statements to the `Program` class:

```
using System;
using NHibernate.Cfg;
using NHibernate.Cfg.Loquacious;
using NHibernate.Dialect;
using NHibernate.Driver;
using NHibernate.Tool.hbm2ddl;
using XmlMappingSample.Domain;
```

15. In the `Main` method of the `Program` class, add code to create a NHibernate configuration object using the fluent configuration API provided by NHibernate, as shown in the following code snippet:

```
var configuration = new Configuration();
configuration.DataBaseIntegration(db =>
{
  db.Dialect<MsSql2008Dialect>();
  db.Driver<SqlClientDriver>();
});
```

16. Note that for this exercise we only need to specify the database type we want to create a schema creation script for.

17. Add code which adds all XML mapping files to the configuration, as shown in the following code snippet:

```
configuration.AddAssembly(typeof (Customer).Assembly);
```

18. Add code to create the SQL schema generation script, as shown in the following code snippet:

```
var exporter = new SchemaExport(configuration);
exporter.Execute(true, false, false);
```

19. Add code to avoid the program exiting without waiting for confirmation, as shown in the following code snippet:

```
Console.Write("Hit enter to exit:");
Console.ReadLine();
```

20. Run the application and analyze the output. The output should look similar to the following screenshot:

```
create table Customer (
    Id INT not null,
    CustomerName NVARCHAR(255) null,
    primary key (Id)
)

create table LineItem (
    Id INT not null,
    Quantity INT null,
    UnitPrice DECIMAL(19,5) null,
    ProductCode NVARCHAR(255) null,
    OrderId INT null,
    primary key (Id)
)

create table Order (
    Id INT not null,
    OrderDate DATETIME null,
    CustomerId INT null,
    primary key (Id)
)

alter table LineItem
    add constraint FKDDD0206AECA664F7
    foreign key (OrderId)
    references Order

alter table Order
    add constraint FK3117099BE516A224
    foreign key (CustomerId)
    references Customer

create table hibernate_unique_key (
    next_hi INT
)

insert into hibernate_unique_key values ( 1 )
Hit enter to exit:
```

What just happened?

In the preceding exercise, we defined the mapping for a simple domain using XML. We added the various XML documents as XML files to the solution and defined their **Build Action** to be **Embedded Resource**. Also, we followed the rule that the filename has to have an extension `*.hbm.xml`.

Finally, we used the `SchemaExport` class of NHibernate to generate the database schema from the mapping.

Pop quiz – XML mapping

1. What are the characteristics of XML mapping?
    a. It is very flexible.
    b. It has only lately been added to NHibernate.
    c. It is terse and highly readable.
    d. It is very verbose.
    e. All of the above.

Summary

In this chapter, we discussed various possibilities to map our domain to an underlying database.

Specifically, we covered:

- The different types of mappings that exist
- How we map entities and their properties to database tables and table columns
- The possibility to influence the mapping process by defining new, or override existing specifications of the mapping framework
- How we can avoid defining explicit mappings altogether
- Using NHibernate to create a SQL schema creation script

Now that we have defined our domain and mapped it to a database, we can move on to discuss the session and transaction objects, which are used to communicate to the database when storing and/or retrieving data.

6
Sessions and Transactions

In this chapter, we will discuss the NHibernate session object which is used to communicate with the database.

In this chapter, we shall:

- Discuss the session and the transaction objects
- Present the session factory object
- Implement an application that saves and retrieves data
- Analyze various methods to manage sessions in the most common application types

So let's get on with it.

What are sessions and transactions

Sessions and transactions are two of the most important objects that the NHibernate framework provides. Through a session object, we are able to communicate with a database and execute various operations on it. A transaction object, in turn, gives us an instrument at hand, which makes managing multiple operations as a unity possible and easy.

Session

Think of a NHibernate session as an abstract or virtual conduit for the database. Gone are the days when you had to create an `ADOConnection`, open the `Connection`, pass the `Connection` to a `Command` object, create a `DataReader` from the `Command` object, and so on.

With NHibernate, we ask the `sessionFactory` for a `Session` object, and that's it. NHibernate handles all of the "real" sessions of the database, connections, pooling, and so on. We reap all the benefits without having to know the underlying intricacies of all of the database backend we are trying to connect to.

Through a session object, we can add new data to the database, update and delete existing data in the database, and also read the existing data from the database. All these operations can be executed in an object-oriented way, without having to deal with SQL strings and the intricacies of a specific database product. A session object allows us to communicate with the data store in a database vendor agnostic way. We do not have to care about whether we are accessing an SQL Server database, a MySQL or Oracle database, and so on. NHibernate completely abstracts those details away for us.

Transaction

A transaction is a concept which allows us to execute a number of tasks as a single unit of work. The outcome of this unit of work is either that all individual steps are successfully executed, or that if at least one of the tasks fails, then the system returns to its original state, as if nothing had ever happened. In this regard, we also talk of an atomic operation.

In ancient history, the Greeks believed that an atom was the smallest particle that existed and that such an atom could not be broken into smaller parts. Similarly, a transaction cannot be partially executed, only as a whole. Individual tasks of a transaction cannot live on their own without causing the system to get into an inconsistent or even invalid state.

A good example for a transaction is the transfer of money from one bank account to another. As a bank customer, money transfer is seen as an atomic operation, although several individual tasks have to be executed until money originating from account A is deposited into account B.

For simplicity, we can assume that the money transfer consists of the following two tasks:

- Task 1: Take 100 US$ out of account A
- Task 2: Put 100 US$ into account B

As the money transfer is a transaction, we can have only two possible outcomes:

1. The transfer succeeds and the balance of account A is reduced by 100 US$, while the balance of account B is increased by 100 US$.
2. The transaction fails and the balance of both accounts A and B remain unchanged.

What does that mean? Well, let's say Task 1 succeeds but Task 2 fails. In such a case, the system has to compensate Task 1 and undo the action. In our case, the system would have to put back the 100 US$ back into account A.

An operation is a transaction if and only if it fulfills the following characteristics. The operation must be:

- Atomic – the operation can only be executed as a whole and not broken apart into smaller units of execution.
- Consistent – the outcome of the operation has to leave the system in a consistent state.
- Isolated – the operation has to run in isolation. The outside world cannot see the result of an unfinished transaction.
- Durable – the outcome of the operation is permanent.

We also use the acronym ACID to describe these characteristics. An operation must be ACID to be a transaction.

The session factory

NHibernate uses a factory object to create new session instances. This factory object is called a session factory. One single session factory object can create as many session objects as desired. The creation of a new session object is a very cheap operation.

On the other hand, the creation of a session factory is very expensive. Depending on the complexity of the system, it can take a considerable amount of time to create a session factory instance. This is the reason why we should only create the session factory once during the whole lifetime of an application.

A session factory is specific to a database. If our application only needs or communicates with a single database, then we need only one session factory. If, on the other hand, our application communicates with several different databases, then we need one session factory object per database.

> In more advanced scenarios, it may well be that we might want to use more than one session factory object, even in the case where we only access one single database. The reasons for this could be that we use more than one schema inside our database and we want to have a session factory per schema; or another reason might be that our application defines several subdomains (often called **bound context**) and we want to access the database from each subdomain through sessions created by a context-specific session factory.

The session factory is thread-safe. Code running on different threads can use the same session factory object to create new session objects. This contrasts with the fact that a session object can only be used in a single thread. In other words: a session object is not thread-safe.

Creating your first session

Creating a NHibernate session is very easy. Once we have a `sessionFactory` object to hand, we can just call the `OpenSession` method on it:

```
var session = sessionFactory.OpenSession();
```

Usually, we might want to open a session in a `using` statement to guarantee that the session is closed and disposed, no matter what the result of the operation is. We might also want to start a transaction for better predictability of the outcome of the operation. Remember, a transaction can either fail as a whole or succeed as a whole; no other outcome is possible. This makes it easier for us to write our application:

```
using (var session = sessionFactory.OpenSession())
{
  using (var transaction = session.BeginTransaction())
  {
    // create, update, delete, or read data

    transaction.Commit();
  }
}
```

Why do we call Commit?

You might have noticed that the above code snippet contains a `transaction.Commit()` statement. Why do we need such a statement? Basically, `Commit` closes our transaction and synchronizes the cached objects with the database. Only after this `Commit` method has been executed successfully are our changes made permanent in the database. Keep in mind that if we don't call `Commit` explicitly and a transaction ends, then all the changes we made are not flushed to the database, and thus not persisted.

We'll talk more about caching in the next session. However, in its simplest configuration, NHibernate uses a first level cache (or the session cache) to store objects. When you first add an object to, or query an object from the database, it is placed into this cache.

If you haven't told NHibernate to update or delete an object from the database, and it has already been cached, then it will pull this object from the cache rather than round-tripping to the database, improving performance.

Adding new data to the database

When creating new entities, we have to call the `Save` method of the NHibernate session object. Only then will NHibernate know about the existence of the respective entity and take care of persisting it to the database. The following statement takes care of this:

```
var newProductId = (int)session.Save(newProduct);
```

Note that the `Save` method returns the ID of the newly generated record. As there are different strategies on how to create an ID (`int` or `long` versus `GUID`), the return type is of type object and we have to type cast the result to the desired and expected type. Instead of using the return value of the `Save` method and casting it to the right type, we can as well access the ID property of the just persisted entity to get the value of the newly generated ID.

```
var newProductId = newProduct.Id;
```

As an alternative to the `Save` method mentioned above, we can also use the `Persist` method of the session object to make a transient entity persistent. The `Persist` method is `void` and we can directly use the ID property of the entity to retrieve the value of the newly generated entity ID. No type casting is needed in this case.

> It is important to note that, at the moment, we use the `Save` or `Persist` method of the session object to make a transient entity persistent. NHibernate is not going to insert anything into the database. Only once the session gets flushed, the corresponding entity is added to the database. The only exception of this is when we use the identity generator to generate the IDs of our entities. In this case, NHibernate has to make a round trip to the database at the moment we call `Save` or `Persist` in order to get the value of the new ID. At the same time, this round trip to the database breaks the concept of the **unit of work**. This is the main reason why it is a recommended best practice NOT to use the identity generator to generateIDs for entities but rather use, for example, the High-Low or one of the GUID generators.

Reading data from the database

To read a single record from the database identified by its primary key value, we can either use the `Get` or the `Load` method of the session object. The following code snippet would load the `Product` entity with ID equal to 1 from the database:

```
var product = session.Get<Product>(1);
```

Thus, in order to use `Get` or `Load`, we have to know the ID of the entity we want to access.

Sessions and Transactions

If we want to load the list of all the stored entities of a given type, then we can use the `Query` (extension) method of the session object. This method is part of the LINQ to NHibernate driver. We will discuss this driver and other means of querying in more details in Chapter 9.

To load the list of all categories, we can use the following code snippet:

```
var allCategories = session.Query<Category>().ToList();
```

Note the `ToList()` call at the end of the statement. LINQ to NHibernate returns a list of type `IQueryable<Category>`, which is lazy evaluated. If we want NHibernate to eagerly load all records, then we can force it to do so by calling `ToList()`.

Get versus Load

At some point, you might wonder why the NHibernate session provides a `Get` and a `Load` method. Do both do the same? If not, which one should I choose?

The fact is that `Get` and `Load` act very differently if lazy loading is enabled. Both the methods are generic in the type of entity to be loaded. That is, if we want to load a `Product` entity, we would use the following code snippet:

```
var product = session.Get<Product>(…);
```

On the other hand, if we want to load a `Customer` entity, then we would use the following code snippet:

```
var customer = session.Get<Customer>(…);
```

The method `Get` expects the primary key value of the desired entity to be passed as a parameter. Thus, to load a product with ID equal to 1, we would use the following code snippet:

```
var product = session.Get<Product>(1);
```

The method `Get` physically retrieves the requested entity from the database if it exists. If the entity with the given ID does NOT exist in the database, then `NULL` is returned.

If we use the method `Load`, then NHibernate does not retrieve the entity from the database, but rather creates a proxy object for us. The only property of this (proxied) entity that is populated with the data is the ID, as NHibernate knows the value because we passed it as a parameter to the method. Thus, when executing the following code:

```
var product = session.Load<Product>(1):
```

[150]

We get a proxied `Product` entity whose ID is equal to 1. The moment our code tries to access any property other than the ID, NHibernate loads the entity from the database. In fact, that is what we call lazy loading, as the database call is deferred to the last possible moment.

> Note that if a `Product` with ID equal to 1 does not exist in the database, NHibernate will still create a proxy for `Product` and populate its ID with the value 1. However, the moment we try to access any other property of the entity, NHibernate would try to hydrate the entity from the database and, as such an entity does not exist, NHibernate would throw an exception.

Given this fact, in which situation would we want to use `Load`? We want to use the `Get` method of the session object whenever we need to access and manipulate the entity. However, we might want to use the `Load` method of the session when we don't really need to change or access the details of an entity. Let's see a simple example that will make things clearer. Assume that we want to update an existing `Product` entity and change its category. A product belongs to a `Category` and thus, the `Product` entity has a property of type `Category`. However, when manipulating products, we don't want to change categories at the same time, only use them. The following code snippet would achieve the desired result:

```
var product = session.Get<Product>(productId);
product.Category = session.Load<Category>(newCategoryId);
```

NHibernate would generate a SELECT statement to load the product, but it would not load the category. It would just create a proxy which we can assign as the new category to the product.

> As the method `Load` does not access the database to verify that the requested category indeed exists, we have to be absolutely sure that the category really exists in the database. Otherwise, NHibernate will throw a foreign key violation exception the moment the session is flushed to the database.

Updating existing data

As the NHibernate session object keeps track of any changes we make to a previously loaded object, we do not have to explicitly call update or any other method of the session object to persist the changes to the database. The moment the session object is flushed, the changes are automatically persisted by NHibernate. That is, the following code snippet would do the trick:

```
using (var session = sessionFactory.OpenSession())
using (var tx = session.BeginTransaction())
{
```

Sessions and Transactions

```
    var product = session.Get<Product>(1);
    product.UnitPrice = 10.55m;
    // new unit price
    tx.Commit();
}
```

Deleting data

To delete an existing record in the database, we have to first load it and can then pass the object to the `Delete` method of the session object, as shown in the following code snippet:

```
var productToDelete = session.Load<Product>(productId);
session.Delete(productToDelete);
```

As the entity is only removed from the database by the above code snippet, but is not itself (yet) deleted from memory, the entity becomes transient again.

Note that, in turn, to not cause unnecessary database round trips, we can use the `Load` method of the session object instead of the `Get` method. The result of the above code snippet is a single SQL delete statement that is sent to the database the moment the session is flushed.

The previous optimization is not applicable in the case that the entity to be deleted contains dependent entities and/or collections of child entities that are mapped with cascading delete constraints. In such a case, NHibernate will have to load the entity into memory.

First level cache or identity map

To achieve better performance, NHibernate intelligently caches data. There are different caching mechanisms in play. The most important one is the first level cache. Each session object maintains such a first level cache. The cache is created when the session object is created and is destroyed when the session object is disposed.

A cache is nothing else but a hashtable. A hashtable stores values by a unique key. A value can be retrieved very efficiently by knowing its key.

NHibernate deals with entities. We have learned what entities are in Chapter 3, when we talked about the model. An entity is uniquely identified by its ID. We have mentioned that two entities are equal if they are of the same type and their IDs match. NHibernate now stipulates that two objects of the same type cannot exist having the same ID. The reason is that if we would allow the system to have two instances with the same ID, then we could put the system in an inconsistent state.

With this boundary condition set so that only one instance of an entity can exist for a given ID, NHibernate can do the following:

An entity is loaded from the database by using its ID. NHibernate puts this entity into the first level cache. The key to access this entity is the value of its ID. When the system tries to load the same entity again from the database, then the session object first consults its cache. If the entity already exists in the cache, then NHibernate returns the cached instance. Only if the cache does not yet contain the entity with the requested ID, does the NHibernate session object load the entity from the database. The following points illustrate in detail what typically happens:

- Application requests a product with ID = 1 from the session
- Session asks the first level cache: "Do you contain product with ID 1?"
- First level cache responds: "No"
- Session loads product with ID 1 from the database
- Session puts product into the first level cache, assigning it as a key for the value of its ID (= 1)
- Session returns product instance to application
- Application executes more operations
- Application again requests a product with ID = 1 from the session
- Session asks first level cache: "Do you contain product with ID 1?"
- First level cache responds: "Yes"
- Session loads product with ID 1 from the cache using the ID as a key and returns it to the application

As the session object uses the ID of the entity as a key to store it in the cache, the first level cache is also called an identity map.

We use the following code to load an entity from the database and implicitly make the NHibernate session store it in its first level cache:

```
var product = sesson.Get<Product>(1);
```

Now each subsequent `Get` does not cause NHibernate to query the database but rather retrieve the object from the first level cache.

Clearing the cache

We can ask the session to remove an entity from the first level cache by using the following statement:

```
session.Evict(product);
```

If we want to completely clean the cache, we can use the following code snippet:

```
session.Clear();
```

The above statements should be used only in very specific situations because, if used incorrectly, they can lead to a significant performance reduction. It is advised that you only ever use these operations when writing test code for the system. We will discuss the details about this in the next chapter.

Refreshing entities in the cache

If we want to refresh a single entity that is already in the first level cache from the database, then we can use the following statement:

```
session.Refresh(product);
```

The preceding code snippet will reload the state of the entity product from the database. This scenario makes sense in the case where the entity has been updated in the database by some other application or process while our session is open.

No database operation without a transaction

Whenever we execute operations that manipulate data in a database, we should wrap these operations inside a transaction:

```
using( var session = sessionFactory.OpenSession())
{
  using (var transaction = session.BeginTransaction())
  {
    // code that manipulates data...
  }
}
```

Each relational database product automatically generates an implicit transaction for us if we do not use our own explicit transaction. This has several drawbacks, one of them being that each single task is a transaction. Multiple tasks cannot be handled as a single unit of work. Additionally, there is also a slight performance penalty to be expected if not using explicit transactions wrapping multiple tasks.

Should I use transactions when querying data?

For optimal performance and predictability of the result, we should also wrap read operations into an explicit transaction. In fact, this is a recommended practice when working with NHibernate.

NHibernate session versus database session

When we are talking of a database session in the context of ADO.NET, we are actually thinking of an open connection to a database through which we can execute various commands, such as retrieve or manipulate data. Such a session lasts as long as the corresponding ADO.NET connection is open. In code, this would look similar to the following code snippet:

```
using (var connection = new SqlConnection("..."))
{
  connection.Open();

  //... write to or read from DB

  connection.Close();
}
```

In NHibernate, a session has a slightly different meaning. We can still think of a NHibernate session being an abstract or virtual conduit to the database. However, this time, there is no need for a physical connection to the database to be established all the time. A NHibernate session can span multiple ADO.NET connections. NHibernate automatically opens an ADO.NET connection to the database only if a write or read operation is taking place.

In this regard, NHibernate alleviates us from the burden to open and close connections, define commands to manipulate data in the database, or to use data readers to query data from the database. A NHibernate session provides us with a higher abstraction and makes working with databases much easier.

A NHibernate session also provides and manages the first level cache which can tremendously improve the performance of an application.

A NHibernate session is a unit of work container, and as such keeps track of all the changes we make to the system.

Sessions and Transactions

Time for action – Creating a session and doing some CRUD

After all this theory, let's now implement a sample. In this exercise, we will define a simple model and use auto-mapping to map the model. We will then create a session factory which provides us with session objects. We will use different session objects to write data to and read data from the database.

1. Open SMSS and log in to your local **.\SQLEXPRESS** database.

2. Define a new empty database called **NHibernateSessionSample**.

3. Open Visual Studio and create a new **Console Application** project. Call the project **NHibernateSessionSample**.

4. To the project, add references to the `NHibernate`, `NHibernate.ByteCode.Castle`, and `FluentNHibernate` assemblies located in the `lib` folder, as shown in the following screenshot:

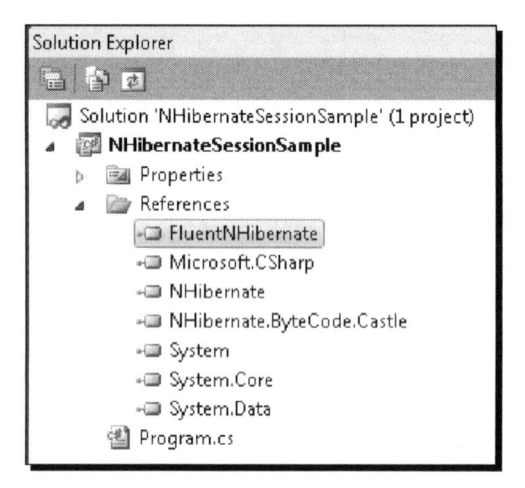

5. Add a folder called `Domain` to the project.

6. Add a class file, `Order`, to the `Domain` folder of the project.

7. Add the following code to the file to define the `Order` entity:

```
public class Order
{
    public virtual int Id { get; set; }
    public virtual Customer Customer { get; set; }
    public virtual DateTime OrderDate { get; set; }
    public virtual IList<LineItem> LineItems { get; set; }
}
```

8. Add a default constructor to the `Order` class and code to initialize the `LineItems` collection, as shown in the following code snippet:

```
public Order()
{
  LineItems = new List<LineItem>();
}
```

9. Add a virtual method to the `Order` class to add a line item, as shown in the following code snippet:

```
public virtual void AddLineItem(int quantity, string productCode)
{
  var item = new LineItem
  {
    Order = this,
    Quantity = quantity,
    ProductCode = productCode
  };
  LineItems.Add(item);
}
```

10. Add a class file, `LineItem` to the `Domain` folder of the project.

11. Add the following code to the file to define the `LineItem` entity:

```
public class LineItem
{
  public virtual int Id { get; set; }
  public virtual Order Order { get; set; }
  public virtual int Quantity { get; set; }
  public virtual string ProductCode { get; set; }
}
```

12. Now add a class file, `Customer` to the `Domain` folder of the project.

13. Add the following code to the file to define the `Customer` entity:

```
public class Customer
{
  public virtual int Id { get; set; }
  public virtual string CustomerName { get; set; }
}
```

14. Add a class file, `OrderingSystemConfiguration` to the project. Add the following code to define which classes the auto-mapper should map:

    ```
    using FluentNHibernate.Automapping;
    using NHibernateSessionSample.Domain;

    public class OrderingSystemConfiguration :
      DefaultAutomappingConfiguration
    {
      public override bool ShouldMap(Type type)
      {
        returntype.Namespace == typeof(Customer).Namespace;
      }
    }
    ```

15. Add code to define a static variable for the session factory in the class `Program`, as shown in the following code snippet:

    ```
    private static ISessionFactory sessionFactory;
    ```

16. Add a static method `ConfigureSystem` to the `Program` class of the project. This method configures NHibernate to use SQL Server as the database. Use auto-mapping to map the domain and automatically create the schema in the database:

    ```
    private static void ConfigureSystem()
    {
    }
    ```

17. Add the following code to define a connection string to the above method:

    ```
    const string connString =
        "server=.\\SQLEXPRESS;database=NHibernateSessionSample;" +
        "integrated security=SSPI;";
    ```

18. Add code to define an instance of the model configuration to the method. This configuration will be used by the auto-mapper, as shown in the following code snippet:

    ```
    var cfg = new OrderingSystemConfiguration();
    ```

19. Add the following code to create an auto-mapping model:

    ```
    var model = AutoMap.AssemblyOf<Customer>(cfg);
    ```

20. Nevertheless, in the same method, use the fluent API to create a NHibernate configuration, as shown in the following code snippet:

    ```
    var configuration = Fluently.Configure()
        .Database(MsSqlConfiguration
    ```

```
        .MsSql2008
        .ConnectionString(connString)
        .ShowSql
    )
    .Mappings(m =>m.AutoMappings.Add(model))
    .BuildConfiguration();
```

21. Note the `.ShowSql` call in the above code snippet. This call configures NHibernate to output all SQL statements it sends to the database to the console.

22. After the preceding code snippet, add code to (re-) create the database schema. Use the `SchemaExport` class of NHibernate and the configuration object just created to do this job, as shown in the following code snippet:

```
var exporter = new SchemaExport(configuration);
exporter.Execute(true, true, false);
```

23. Finally, use the `configuration` object to create the session factory, as shown in the following code snippet:

```
sessionFactory = configuration.BuildSessionFactory();
```

24. Add a static method `CreateCustomers` to the `Program` class. This method creates two customer objects with some pre-canned data and stores them in the database by using the session object, as shown in the following code snippet:

```
private static void CreateCustomers()
{
   var customerA = new Customer {CustomerName = "Microsoft"};
   var customerB = new Customer {CustomerName = "Apple Computer"};

   using (var session = sessionFactory.OpenSession())
   using (var transaction = session.BeginTransaction())
   {
      session.Save(customerA);
      session.Save(customerB);
      transaction.Commit();
   }
}
```

25. Note that we use a transaction to wrap the saving of the two customers in the database. The transaction is made permanent by calling `Commit` from the transaction object.

Sessions and Transactions

26. Add code to the Main method of the Program class to configure the system and create some customer objects. Furthermore, add code so that the program asks for confirmation prior to ending, as shown in the following code snippet:

```
static void Main()
{
  ConfigureSystem();
  CreateCustomers();

  Console.Write("\r\nHit enter to exit:");
  Console.ReadLine();
}
```

27. Run the application and try to understand the output generated in the console window. The output should look similar to the following screenshot:

28. The first couple of lines show the SQL commands to clean out the schema if it already exists, followed by the SQL scripts to generate the new schema. Finally, at the end of the screen, we have the two insert statements which create the customer records in the database.

Next, we want to create an order with some line items and which is associated with an existing customer. We will see how NHibernate, if configured correctly, automatically cascades the insert operation to the line item children and that we do not need to explicitly save the line items.

29. Add a private static method `CreateOrder` to the `Program` class, as shown in the following code snippet:

```
private static int CreateOrder()
{
}
```

30. Add code to this method to create a `customer` object and an `order` with line items using precanned data, as shown in the following code snippet:

```
var customer = new Customer {CustomerName = "Intel"};
var order = new Order
{
   Customer = customer,
   OrderDate = DateTime.Now,
};
order.AddLineItem(1, "Apple");
order.AddLineItem(5, "Pear");
order.AddLineItem(3, "Banana");
```

31. Now add code to save the `customer` and the `order` object in the database, as shown in the following code snippet:

```
int orderId;
using (var session = sessionFactory.OpenSession())
using (var transaction = session.BeginTransaction())
{
   session.Save(customer);
   orderId = (int)session.Save(order);
   transaction.Commit();
}
```

32. Return the ID of the newly generated order to the caller, as shown in the following code:

```
return orderId;
```

Sessions and Transactions

33. In the `Main` method, just after the call to `CreateCustomers`, add code to call the `CreateOrder` function, as shown in the following code:

```
var orderId = CreateOrder();
```

34. Run the application. Note that the application terminates with an exception with the following message:
NHibernate.TransientObjectException"object references an unsaved transient instance - save the transient instance before flushing. Type: NHibernateSessionSample.Domain.LineItem, Entity: NHibernateSessionSample. Domain.LineItem"

35. We have to override the default configuration of the auto-mapper regarding how it maps the `HasMany` part of the order entity. By default, auto-mapper configures `HasMany` relations as non-inverse and cascade equal to none. To configure the mapping as we want it, add the following code right after the definition of the auto-mapper model in the `ConfigureSystem` method (that is after the line `var model = AutoMap.AssemblyOf<Customer>(cfg);`):

```
model.Override<Order>(
    map =>map.HasMany(x =>x.LineItems)
    .Inverse()
    .Cascade.AllDeleteOrphan()
    );
```

36. Run the application again and you should see the output as shown in the following screenshot:

```
NHibernate: INSERT INTO [Customer] (CustomerName) VALUES (@p0); select SCOPE_IDE
NTITY();@p0 = 'Intel' [Type: String (4000)]
NHibernate: INSERT INTO [Order] (OrderDate, Customer_id) VALUES (@p0, @p1); sele
ct SCOPE_IDENTITY();@p0 = 2/26/2011 9:52:30 PM [Type: DateTime (0)], @p1 = 3 [Ty
pe: Int32 (0)]
NHibernate: INSERT INTO [LineItem] (Quantity, ProductCode, Order_id) VALUES (@p0
, @p1, @p2); select SCOPE_IDENTITY();@p0 = 1 [Type: Int32 (0)], @p1 = 'Apple' [T
ype: String (4000)], @p2 = 1 [Type: Int32 (0)]
NHibernate: INSERT INTO [LineItem] (Quantity, ProductCode, Order_id) VALUES (@p0
, @p1, @p2); select SCOPE_IDENTITY();@p0 = 5 [Type: Int32 (0)], @p1 = 'Pear' [Ty
pe: String (4000)], @p2 = 1 [Type: Int32 (0)]
NHibernate: INSERT INTO [LineItem] (Quantity, ProductCode, Order_id) VALUES (@p0
, @p1, @p2); select SCOPE_IDENTITY();@p0 = 3 [Type: Int32 (0)], @p1 = 'Banana' [
Type: String (4000)], @p2 = 1 [Type: Int32 (0)]
```

37. Note that the three line items of the order are automatically added to the database without us specifying it explicitly.

Chapter 6

Now we want to load an existing order and remove one of its line items and add a new one in its place.

38. Add a new method `UpdateOrder` to the `Program` class, as shown in the following code snippet:

```
private static void UpdateOrder(int orderId)
{
}
```

39. Add code to create a new session and start a new transaction, as shown in the following code snippet:

```
using (var session = sessionFactory.OpenSession())
using (var transaction = session.BeginTransaction())
{
}
```

40. Inside this new transaction, add code to load the order from the database that we have previously generated, as shown in the following code snippet:

```
var order = session.Get<Order>(orderId);
```

41. Add code to remove the first line item of the order:

```
order.LineItems.RemoveAt(0);
```

42. Now add code to add a new line item to the order:

```
order.AddLineItem(2, "Apricot");
```

43. Commit the transaction, as shown in the following code snippet:

```
transaction.Commit();
```

44. To the `Main` method of the `Program` class, add a call to this new `UpdateOrder` method:

```
UpdateOrder(orderId);
```

45. Run the application. The end of the output in the console window should look similar to the following screenshot:

```
NHibernate: SELECT order0_.Id as Id2_0_, order0_.OrderDate as OrderDate2_0_, ord
er0_.Customer_id as Customer3_2_0_ FROM [Order] order0_ WHERE order0_.Id=@p0;@p0
 = 1 [Type: Int32 (0)]
NHibernate: SELECT lineitems0_.Order_id as Order4_1_, lineitems0_.Id as Id1_, li
neitems0_.Id as Id1_0_, lineitems0_.Quantity as Quantity1_0_, lineitems0_.Produc
tCode as ProductC3_1_0_, lineitems0_.Order_id as Order4_1_0_ FROM [LineItem] lin
eitems0_ WHERE lineitems0_.Order_id=@p0;@p0 = 1 [Type: Int32 (0)]
NHibernate: INSERT INTO [LineItem] (Quantity, ProductCode, Order_id) VALUES (@p0
, @p1, @p2); select SCOPE_IDENTITY();@p0 = 2 [Type: Int32 (0)], @p1 = 'Apricot'
[Type: String (4000)], @p2 = 1 [Type: Int32 (0)]
NHibernate: DELETE FROM [LineItem] WHERE Id = @p0;@p0 = 1 [Type: Int32 (0)]
```

Sessions and Transactions

46. The first select statement loads the order. The second select statement loads the line items of the order. Lastly, we see an insert statement, which adds the new line item to the database. And last, we have the delete statement, which removes the deleted line item from the database.

Last but not least, let's delete the order. We expect that all the line items of the order will also be deleted by NHibernate without us having to specify it.

1. Add a new method `DeleteOrder` to the `Program` class:

   ```
   private static void DeleteOrder(int orderId)
   {
   }
   ```

2. Add code to create a new session and start a new transaction, as shown in the following code snippet:

   ```
   using (var session = sessionFactory.OpenSession())
   using (var transaction = session.BeginTransaction())
   {
   }
   ```

3. Inside this new transaction, add code to load the order from the database that we have previously generated:

   ```
   var order = session.Load<Order>(orderId);
   ```

4. Add code to remove `order` from the system, as shown in the following code snippet:

   ```
   session.Delete(order);
   ```

5. Do not forget to commit the deletion of the order, as shown in the following code snippet:

   ```
   transaction.Commit();
   ```

6. Now, add code to the `Main` method to call this `DeleteOrder` method, as shown in the following code snippet:

   ```
   DeleteOrder(orderId);
   ```

7. Run the application. The end of the output in the console window should look similar to the following screenshot:

```
NHibernate: SELECT order0_.Id as Id2_0_, order0_.OrderDate as OrderDate2_0_, ord
er0_.Customer_id as Customer3_2_0_ FROM [Order] order0_ WHERE order0_.Id=@p0;@p0
 = 1 [Type: Int32 (0)]
NHibernate: SELECT lineitems0_.Order_id as Order4_1_, lineitems0_.Id as Id1_, li
neitems0_.Id as Id1_0_, lineitems0_.Quantity as Quantity1_0_, lineitems0_.Produc
tCode as ProductC3_1_0_, lineitems0_.Order_id as Order4_1_0_ FROM [LineItem] lin
eitems0_ WHERE lineitems0_.Order_id=@p0;@p0 = 1 [Type: Int32 (0)]
NHibernate: DELETE FROM [LineItem] WHERE Id = @p0;@p0 = 2 [Type: Int32 (0)]
NHibernate: DELETE FROM [LineItem] WHERE Id = @p0;@p0 = 3 [Type: Int32 (0)]
NHibernate: DELETE FROM [LineItem] WHERE Id = @p0;@p0 = 4 [Type: Int32 (0)]
NHibernate: DELETE FROM [Order] WHERE Id = @p0;@p0 = 1 [Type: Int32 (0)]
```

8. The first select statement loads the order, the second one loads the line items of the order. All the line items of the order are deleted before the order itself is deleted.

What just happened?

We have created a simple domain model and used Fluent NHibernate's auto-mapping to map the domain to the underlying database schema. With the help of the `SchemaExport` class of NHibernate, we then created the database schema from the mapping.

We then created a session object and used it to create the `Customer`, `Order`, and `LineItem` entries in the respective database tables. Subsequently, we used the session object to update and also delete existing records in the database.

Pop quiz – Creating, updating, and deleting data

1. You want to create a new session. What object do you use?
    a. I need no other object; I just create a new session instance by using the **new** keyword.
    b. The NHibernate configuration object.
    c. The session factory object.
    d. None of the above.

2. Which method of the session object can you use to add a new object to the database?
    a. session.Update(...)
    b. session.SaveOrUpdate(...)
    c. session.Save(...)
    d. session.New(...)

3. How do you remove a record from the database?
    a. session.Remove(...)
    b. session.Clear(...)
    c. session.Delete(...)
    d. transaction.Commit()

Session management

When developing applications on .NET, you will probably, sooner or later, have to deal with one or several of the following three types of applications:

1. Web-based applications, including Silverlight applications.
2. WinForm or WPF applications.
3. Windows services.

There are, of course, many other types of applications, but they can all probably use the same approach regarding NHibernate session management as one of the three types mentioned above.

Web-based applications

Because of the stateless nature of web applications, we cannot (and should not!) try to maintain and use a single session across multiple page requests. However, as the creation of a session object is a very cheap operation, this should not be a problem per se. On the other hand, we have to remember that creating a session factory can be very expensive. Thus, the session factory should only be created once during the life cycle of the web application. It turns out that creating the session factory during the application start-up is probably the best way to do it.

The session factory is thread-safe, which is very important in web-based applications, as every single web request can happen on a different thread.

After creation, the session factory can, for example, be stored in the ASP.NET application object, which makes it available globally throughout the whole application.

One of the most commonly used patterns for NHibernate sessions is the session per request pattern. A new session object is created at the beginning of a new web request. The session object is then flushed and disposed at the end of the web request.

It is highly recommended to use an IoC container to manage and configure objects when implementing a web application. Having an IoC container at hand, we would store the session object in the container, and in this way, make it available to all other objects through dependency injection. However, for this introduction, it is assumed that we have no IoC container at hand. Thus, let's provide a solution for this case. We will use the **singleton pattern** to implement a session provider.

Time for action – Implementing session management for a web application

In this sample, we will create a simple Silverlight application and implement a basic session management for this application. A Silverlight application is a web-based application, and thus the techniques learned here can be applied to any other type of web application (for example, ASP.NET MVC or WebForms).

1. Open SSMS and log in to your local **.\SQLEXPRESS** database server.
2. Create a new database called **SilverlightSample**.
3. Open Visual Studio and create a new project.
4. Select **Silverlight Application** as the project template and call the project **SilverlightSample**, as shown in the following screenshot:

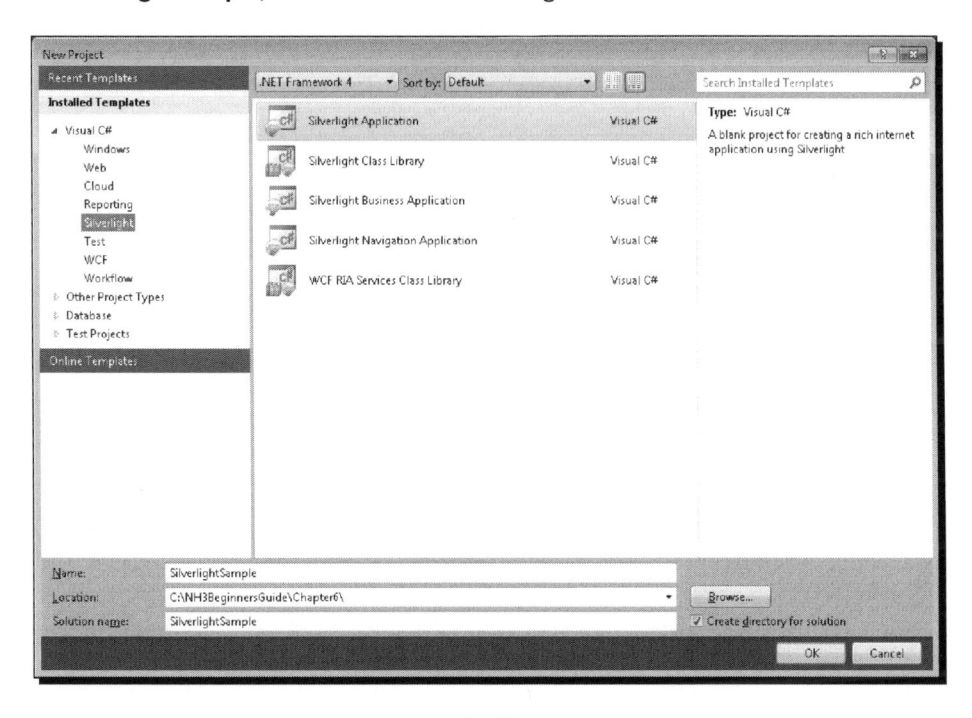

5. When asked whether to host the Silverlight application in a new website, leave all the defaults, as shown in the following screenshot, and click on **OK** to continue.

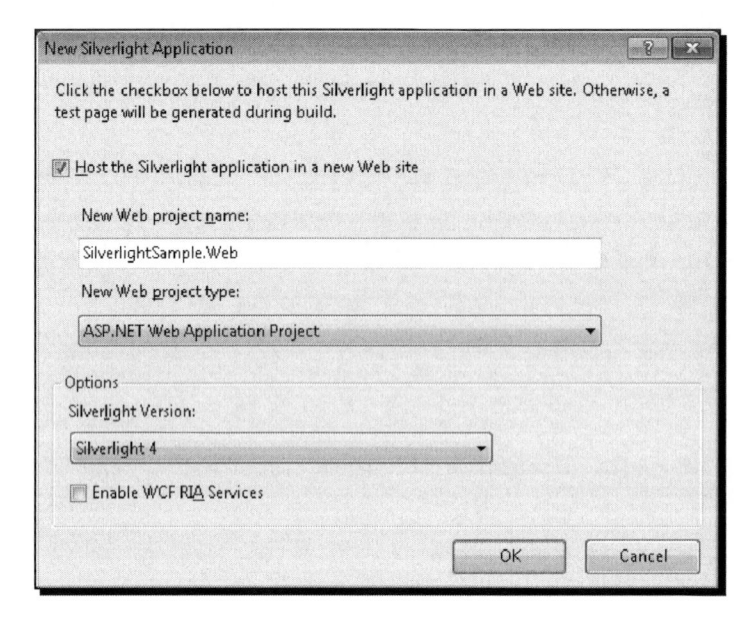

6. To the `SilverlightSample.Web` project, add references to the three assemblies, `NHibernate`, `NHibernate.ByteCode.Castle`, and `FluentNHibernate`, located in the `lib` folder.

7. Add the class file `Product.cs` to the web project (`SilverlightSample.Web`) and add code to define a simple `Product` entity, as shown in the following code snippet:
   ```
   public class Product
   {
     public virtual int Id { get; set; }
     public virtual string Name { get; set; }
   }
   ```

8. Now add a class file `ProductMap.cs` to the web project to define the mapping of the `Product` entity, as shown in the following code snippet:
   ```
   public class ProductMap : ClassMap<Product>
   {
     public ProductMap()
     {
       Id(x =>x.Id).GeneratedBy.HiLo("1000");
       Map(x =>x.Name);
     }
   }
   ```

9. Add a class `SessionProvider` to the `SilverlightSample.Web` project. This class has a `static` property of type `SessionProvider` called `Instance`. The property has a private setter that cannot be changed from outside the class, as shown in the following code snippet:

```
public class SessionProvider
{
   public static SessionProvider Instance { get; private set; }
}
```

10. Add a static instance variable of type `ISessionFactory` to the class, as shown in the following code snippet:

```
private static ISessionFactory sessionFactory;
```

11. Add a `static` constructor to the class which initializes the `Instance` property, as shown in the following code snippet:

```
static SessionProvider()
{
   var provider = new SessionProvider();
   provider.Initialize();
   Instance = provider;
}
```

12. Add an empty `private` constructor to the class that cannot be instantiated, as shown in the following code snippet:

```
private SessionProvider()
{
}
```

13. Add an `Initialize` method to the class which contains the code to configure NHibernate, (re)create the database schema, and create a session factory:

```
private void Initialize()
{
   const string connString =
      "server=.\\SQLEXPRESS;database=SilverlightSample;" +
      "user id=sa;password=sa;";

   var configuration = Fluently.Configure()
      .Database(MsSqlConfiguration.MsSql2008
      .ConnectionString(connString)
      .ShowSql())
      .Mappings(m =>m.FluentMappings
      .AddFromAssemblyOf<Product>())
      .BuildConfiguration();
```

Sessions and Transactions

```
    var exporter = new SchemaExport(configuration);
    exporter.Execute(true, true, false);

    sessionFactory = configuration.BuildSessionFactory();
}
```

14. Note that this time, in the definition of the connection string, we don't use integrated security but rather a user ID/password combination. Make sure that you use a combination which has the appropriate rights on your SQL Server Express database.

15. Add a public method `OpenSession`, which returns `ISession` to the class. This method uses the session factory to get a new session object and return it to the caller:

```
public ISession OpenSession()
{
   return sessionFactory.OpenSession();
}
```

16. Add a **Silverlight-enabled WCF Service** to the web project. Call the service **ProductService**, as shown in the following screenshot:

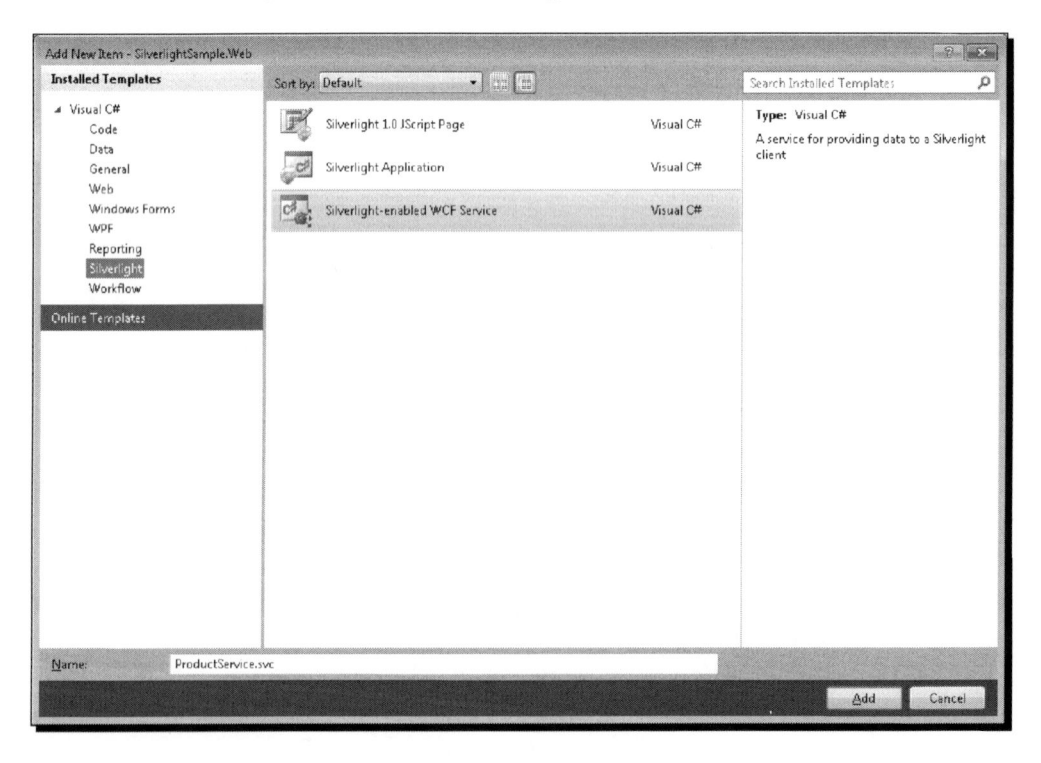

17. Delete the default method in the class and add a method `CreateProduct`, which has a return type of `int`:

```
[OperationContract]
public int CreateProduct()
{
}
```

18. Add code to the method to create a product, open a new session, start a new transaction, and save the product to the database. Return the ID of the newly created product. The service should look similar to the following code snippet:

```
using System.ServiceModel;
using System.ServiceModel.Activation;

namespace SilverlightSample.Web
{
  [ServiceContract(Namespace = "")]
  [AspNetCompatibilityRequirements(RequirementsMode =
    AspNetCompatibilityRequirementsMode.Allowed)]
  public class ProductService
  {
    [OperationContract]
    public int CreateProduct()
    {
      using (var session = SessionProvider
        .Instance.OpenSession())
      using (var transaction = session.BeginTransaction())
      {
        var product = new Product {Name = "Apple"};
        var productId = (int)session.Save(product);
        transaction.Commit();
        return productId;
      }
    }
  }
}
```

19. Note that when adding the WCF service to the web project, Visual Studio automatically updated the `Web.config` file of the project to configure an endpoint for this new WCF service. You can leave these default values as they are and the application will work.

20. Compile the solution. This step is important for the next steps to work properly!

Sessions and Transactions

21. In the **Solution Explorer** window, right-click on the **SilverlightSample** project and select **Add Service Reference...**.

22. In the **Add Service Reference** dialog window, click on the **Discover** button.

23. Visual Studio should discover the **ProductService.svc** service on the local machine. Expand the **ProductService.svc** node in the **Services** list, as shown in the following screenshot:

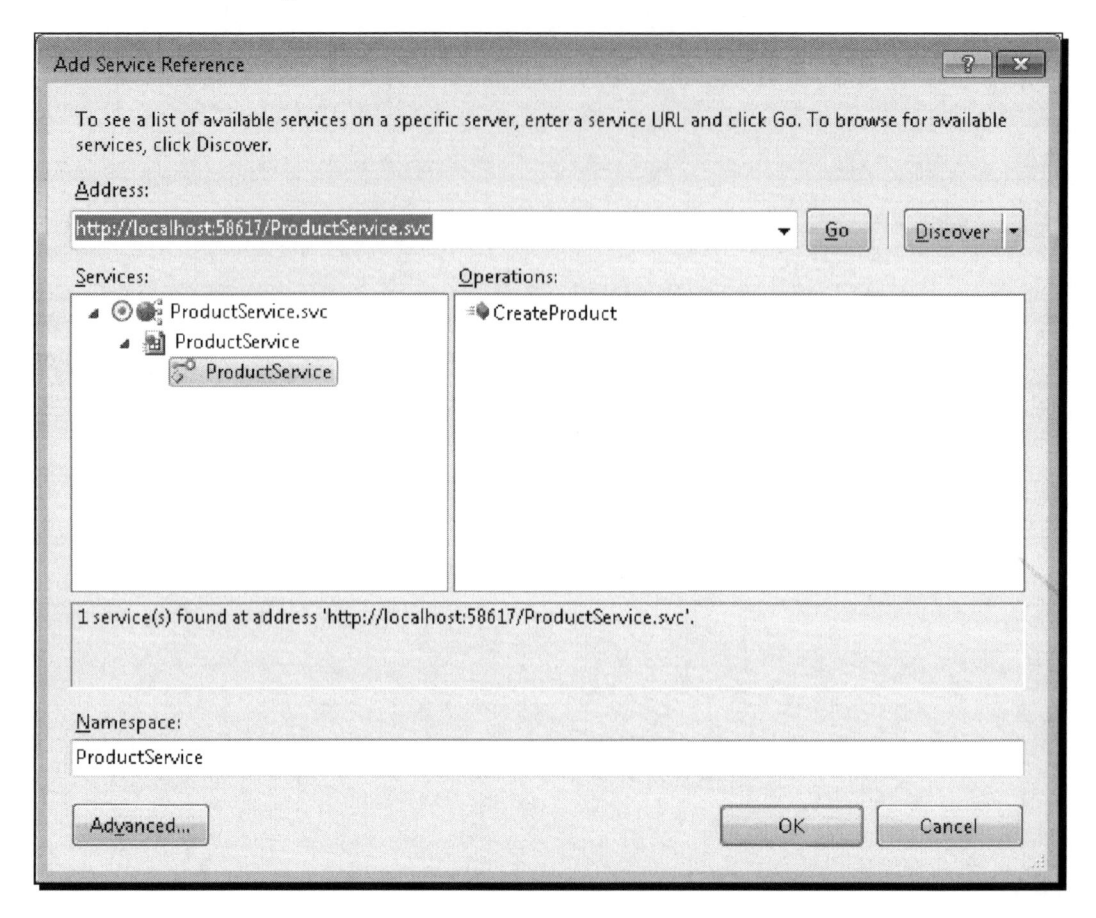

24. Note that, by default, the **Namespace** is defined as **ServiceReference1**. Change this to **ProductService**.

25. Click on **OK** to continue. Visual Studio will create a proxy to the web service, which can be used by the client (the Silverlight application), as shown in the following screenshot:

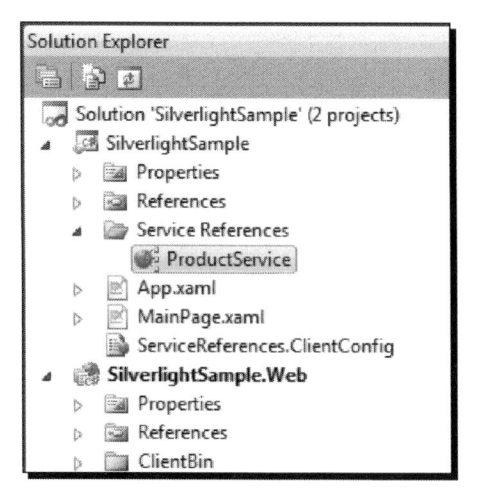

26. In the **SilverlightSample** project, add code to the **MainPage.xaml** to create a button, as shown in the following code snippet:

```
<UserControl x:Class="SilverlightSample.MainPage"
xmlns="http://schemas.microsoft.com/winfx/2006/xaml
  /presentation"
xmlns:x="http://schemas.microsoft.com/winfx/2006/xaml"
xmlns:d="http://schemas.microsoft.com/expression/blend/2008"
xmlns:mc="http://schemas.openxmlformats.org/markup-
  compatibility/2006"
mc:Ignorable="d"d:DesignHeight="300" d:DesignWidth="400">

<Grid x:Name="LayoutRoot" Background="White">
   <Button x:Name="CreateProduct" Content="Create Product"
     Click="OnCreateProduct" Width="100" Height="30"/>
</Grid>
</UserControl>
```

27. Add code to the `Click` event handler in the preceding code snippet (the `MainPage.xaml.cs` file), which uses the `ProductService` proxy to create a product in the database, as shown in the following code snippet:

```
private void OnCreateProduct(object sender, RoutedEventArgs e)
{
   var client = new ProductServiceClient();
   client.CreateProductCompleted += OnProductCreated;
```

Sessions and Transactions

```
    client.CreateProductAsync();
}

private void OnProductCreated(object sender,
    CreateProductCompletedEventArgs e)
{
    MessageBox.Show(string.Format(
      "Created product with id={0}", e.Result));
}
```

28. Run the application and click on the **CreateProduct** button. The application should respond with a message box similar to the following screenshot:

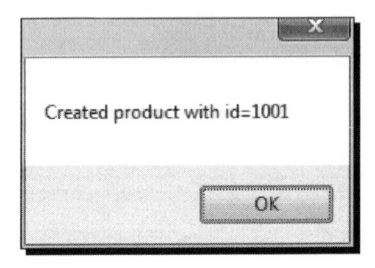

> Created product with id=1001
>
> OK

What just happened?

We created a basic session provider which can be used in a web-based application such as an ASP.NET MVC, WebForms, or Silverlight application. Web applications are stateless in nature and we have used the singleton pattern to deal with this fact, and have a means to easily create sessions.

WinForm or WPF applications

These types of applications are what we call state-full and it is "easier" to manage sessions in these scenarios. Usually, we would want to open a session per screen and keep the session open as long as the screen is open. If you are using a Model-View-Presenter (MVP) pattern for your application, then the presenter would be responsible for managing the session.

Keep in mind though that if an exception happens during the lifetime of a screen, then the NHibernate session is in an inconsistent state and cannot be used any further. You will have to close this session and open a new one.

Windows services

In a Windows service, we typically create the session factory when the service starts and we dispose the factory when the service stops. The decision of when a session has to be created depends on the nature of the database communication of the service. Most probably, we would want to create a session whenever we need to execute a (business) transaction.

Unit of Work

When we load objects from the database and change them, it is important to keep track of what we have changed; otherwise, the changed objects won't be written to the database. Furthermore, new objects have to be added to the database and objects we delete have to be removed from the database.

A **Unit of Work** (UoW) is used to keep track of everything that happens during a business transaction and that affects the database. It keeps track of every single step needed to update the database once the business transaction is completed. The UoW guarantees that the individual database operations needed to update the system are executed in the right order, to avoid any database constraint violations.

In NHibernate, we have the `Session` object, which is a UoW container. The session object keeps track of all objects we load, new objects we add, existing objects we delete, and changes we make to any of these objects. Only when the session is being flushed will the database be altered. (That is, only then will the necessary create, update, and delete statements be sent to the database.)

Handling exception

We can put it very short and simply: all NHibernate exceptions are **non-recoverable**!

NHibernate use might lead to exceptions, usually, `HibernateException`. This exception can have a nested inner exception. To access the root cause of the exception, we can and should use the `InnerException` property.

If an exception happens during a database operation, then the NHibernate session object is in an inconsistent state and should NOT be used any more. It is best to immediately rollback the active transaction, dispose the current session, and start over. Here is a code snippet we can use to deal with the possibility of exception happening:

```
var session = sessionFactory.OpenSession();
var transaction = session.BeginTransaction();
try
{
  // do some work
  ...
  transaction.Commit();
}
catch (Exception e)
{
  transaction.Rollback();
```

```
      throw;
   }
   finally
   {
      session.Close();
   }
```

Second level cache

We have seen that NHibernate provides a very efficient way to cache data. Unfortunately, this first level cache is bound to a session object. This means that each time a session is disposed, all the cached data is lost. Sometimes, we need to be a little bit more flexible. We might want to cache some data not just for the duration of a session's lifetime, but rather globally, and make it available to all session objects. For such scenarios, NHibernate introduces the concept of the second level cache.

The second level cache is defined per session factory and lives as long as the session factory is not disposed. Once an entity is loaded by its unique ID and the second level cache is active, the entity is available for all other sessions (of the same session factory). Thus, once the entity is in the second level cache, NHibernate won't load the entity from the database until it is removed from the cache.

To enable the second level cache, we have to define which cache provider we want to use. There exist various implementations of a second level cache. For our sample, we use a hashtable-based cache, which is included in the core NHibernate assembly. Please note that you should never use this cache provider for production level code, only for testing. Please refer to the section *Second level cache implementations* below, to decide which implementation best fits your needs; though you won't have to change your code if you change the cache provider.

Using code similar to the following code snippet would cause NHibernate to only access the database once to retrieve the product with ID 1, although we use two different session instances:

```
using (var session1 = sessionFactory.OpenSession())
{
   var product = session1.Get<Product>(1);
}

using (var session2 = sessionFactory.OpenSession())
{
   var product = session2.Get<Product>(1);
}
```

The second `Get` operation would take the product entity out of the second level cache.

Note, however, that without having the second level cache enabled, the above code would result in two requests to the database as the first level cache of each session cannot be used by any other session.

Additionally, note that to enable the second level cache, we have to configure NHibernate accordingly. The details of this configuration will be explained in Chapter 8. We also have to define the mapping of the entity that it is cacheable. If we are using fluent mappings provided by Fluent NHibernate to map our entities, then the necessary statement to add to the mapping would be:

```
Cache.ReadWrite();
```

Only entities that are explicitly configured will be cached in the second level cache.

Cache regions

If we don't use cache regions, then the second level cache can only be cleared as a whole. If we need to clear only part of the second level cache then we use regions. Regions are distinguished by their name. We can put any number of different queries into a named cache region. The command to clear a cache region is as follows:

```
sessionFactory.EvictQueries("My Region");
```

`sessionFactory` is the session factory instance currently used and `My Region` is the name of the cache region.

Second level cache implementations

All second level cache providers are part of the NHibernate contributions project. The following list gives a short description of some of the supported providers.

- SysCache: Uses `System.Web.Caching.Cache` as the cache provider. This means that you can rely on the ASP.NET caching feature to understand how it works.
- SysCache2: Similar to `NHibernate.Caches.SysCache`, uses ASP.NET cache. This provider also supports SQL dependency-based expiration, meaning that it is possible to configure certain cache regions to automatically expire when the relevant data in the database changes.
- Velocity: Caching provider, which is part of Microsoft Windows Server App Fabric, which in turn is a set of integrated services to build, scale, and manage IIS-based web applications.

Sessions and Transactions

- **Prevalence**: Uses `Bamboo.Prevalence` as the cache provider. `Bamboo.Prevalence` is a .NET implementation of the object prevalence concept brought to life by Klaus Wuestefeld in Prevayler. `Bamboo.Prevalence` provides transparent object persistence to deterministic systems targeting the CLR. It offers persistent caching for smart client applications.

- **MemCache**: Uses Memcached. Memcached is a high-performance, distributed memory object caching system, generic in nature, but intended for use in speeding up dynamic web applications by alleviating database load. Basically, a distributed hash table.

Time for action – Using a second level cache

In this exercise, we want to implement a very simple application which uses NHibernate's second level cache. We use the hashtable cache provider in this exercise, but please make sure that you are never using this provider in the production level code!

1. Open SSMS and log in to your local SQL Express database.
2. Add a new database named `SecondLevelCacheSample` to the database server.
3. Open Visual Studio and create a new **Console Application** named `SecondLevelCacheSample`.
4. Add references to the `NHibernate.dll`, `FluentNHibernate.dll`, and `NHibernate.ByteCode.Castle.dll` assemblies located in the `lib` folder.
5. Create a folder `Domain` in the Project.
6. Add a class file, `Product.cs`, to the `Domain` folder of the project.
7. Add the following code to the class to define the `Product` entity, as shown in the following code snippet:

    ```
    public class Product
    {
       public virtual int Id { get; set; }
       public virtual string Name { get; set; }
       public virtual decimal UnitPrice { get; set; }
       public virtual int ReorderLevel { get; set; }
       public virtual bool Discontinued { get; set; }
    }
    ```

8. Add a class file, `ProductMap.cs` to the `Domain` folder of the project. This will be the mapping file for the `Product` entity:

9. The mapping file shall contain the following code:
```
public class ProductMap : ClassMap<Product>
{
  publicProductMap()
  {
    Cache.ReadWrite();

    Id(x =>x.Id).GeneratedBy.HiLo("1000");
    Map(x =>x.Name);
    Map(x =>x.UnitPrice);
    Map(x =>x.ReorderLevel);
    Map(x =>x.Discontinued);
  }
}
```

10. Now that we have added a `Cache.ReadWrite()` statement to the mapping, this instructs NHibernate to use the second level cache for the `Product` entity.

11. Add a static field of type `ISessionFactory` to the `Program` class, as shown in the following code snippet:
```
private static ISessionFactory sessionFactory;
```

12. Add a static method `ConfigureSystem` to the `Program` class. This method will contain the code to configure NHibernate in general, and specifically the second level cache; as shown in the following code snippet:
```
private static void ConfigureSystem()
{
}
```

13. Add the following code to define a connection string to the database `SecondLevelCacheSample` we defined in step 2:
```
const string connString=
    "server=.\\SQLEXPRESS;database=SecondLevelCacheSample;" +
    "integrated security=SSPI;";
```

14. Use the fluent API of Fluent NHibernate to define a NHibernate configuration object, as shown in the following code snippet:
```
var configuration = Fluently.Configure()
    .Database(MsSqlConfiguration.MsSql2008
    .ConnectionString(connString)
    .ShowSql)
    .Mappings(m =>m.FluentMappings
    .AddFromAssemblyOf<Product>())
    .BuildConfiguration();
```

Sessions and Transactions

15. Add code that extends the configuration to use the second level cache, as shown in the following code snippet:

    ```
    configuration.Properties["cache.provider_class"] =
       "NHibernate.Cache.HashtableCacheProvider";
    configuration.Properties["cache.use_second_level_cache"] =
       "true";
    ```

16. The first value tells NHibernate which second level cache provider to use. It is a key value pair. The value is the full path to the class which implements the second level cache provider. In our sample, we do not need to define the assembly, as the provider we chose resides in the NHibernate assembly.

17. The second value enables or disables the usage of the second level cache, depending on the setting. Note that, technically, this second setting is not needed as the value is equal to true by default.

18. Now, add code to the `ConfigureSystem` method, which (re)creates the database schema by using the `SchemaExport` class of NHibernate, as shown in the following code snippet:

    ```
    var exporter = new SchemaExport(configuration);
    exporter.Execute(true, true, false);
    ```

19. Finally, still to the same method, add code to generate a session factory from the configuration object, as shown in the following code:

    ```
    sessionFactory = configuration.BuildSessionFactory();
    ```

20. In the `Program` class, create a `static` method `TestLoadEntity`, as shown in the following code snippet:

    ```
    private static void TestLoadEntity()
    {
    }
    ```

21. In the preceding method, implement code to create a `product` instance and save it in the database, as shown in the following code snippet:

    ```
    int productId;
    var product = new Product
    {
      Name = "Apple",
      UnitPrice = 1.55m,
      ReorderLevel = 100,
      Discontinued = false
    };
    using (var session = sessionFactory.OpenSession())
    ```

```
using (var tx = session.BeginTransaction())
{
  productId = (int) session.Save(product);
  tx.Commit();
}
```

22. To the same method, add code which opens two different sessions and, through each session, loads the product just stored by the preceding code fragment, as shown in the following code snippet:

```
using (var session1 = sessionFactory.OpenSession())
{
  var product1 = session1.Get<Product>(productId);
}

using (var session2 = sessionFactory.OpenSession())
{
  var product2 = session2.Get<Product>(productId);
}
```

23. Add code to the Main method in the Program class, which calls the ConfigureSystem and the TestLoadEntity methods, and asks the user to hit *Enter* to exit the application:

```
static void Main()
{
  ConfigureSystem();
  TestLoadEntity();

  Console.Write("\r\nHit enter to exit:");
  Console.ReadLine();
}
```

24. Run the application and verify that no select statement is generated by NHibernate. This shows us that the second level cache is indeed in action. The (last part of the) output on the console should look similar to the following screenshot:

```
NHibernate: INSERT INTO [Product] (Name, UnitPrice, ReorderLevel, Discontinued,
 Id) VALUES (@p0, @p1, @p2, @p3, @p4);@p0 = 'Apple' [Type: String (4000)], @p1 =
 1.55 [Type: Decimal (0)], @p2 = 100 [Type: Int32 (0)], @p3 = False [Type: Boolea
n (0)], @p4 = 1001 [Type: Int32 (0)]
Hit enter to exit:
```

25. We just have the insert statement, which creates the product in the database, but no select statement to read the product from the database.

26. Now, change the `cache.use_second_level_cache` setting to `false` and run the program again. This time, two select statements should be sent to the database; one for each session, as shown in the following screenshot:

```
NHibernate: INSERT INTO [Product] (Name, UnitPrice, ReorderLevel, Discontinued,
Id) VALUES (@p0, @p1, @p2, @p3, @p4);@p0 = 'Apple' [Type: String (4000)], @p1 =
1.55 [Type: Decimal (0)], @p2 = 100 [Type: Int32 (0)], @p3 = False [Type: Boolea
n (0)], @p4 = 1001 [Type: Int32 (0)]
NHibernate: SELECT product0_.Id as Id0_0_, product0_.Name as Name0_0_, product0_
.UnitPrice as UnitPrice0_0_, product0_.ReorderLevel as ReorderL4_0_0_, product0_
.Discontinued as Disconti5_0_0_ FROM [Product] product0_ WHERE product0_.Id=@p0;
@p0 = 1001 [Type: Int32 (0)]
NHibernate: SELECT product0_.Id as Id0_0_, product0_.Name as Name0_0_, product0_
.UnitPrice as UnitPrice0_0_, product0_.ReorderLevel as ReorderL4_0_0_, product0_
.Discontinued as Disconti5_0_0_ FROM [Product] product0_ WHERE product0_.Id=@p0;
@p0 = 1001 [Type: Int32 (0)]

Hit enter to exit:
```

27. Obviously, in addition to the insert statement, we have two select statements: one for each session object used to load the product entity.

What just happened?

In the previous exercise, we have learned how to configure our application such that NHibernate uses a second level cache. We also saw how to configure the mapping of our entities such that they can be cached by NHibernate in the second level cache. We also realized that, with a single switch, we can turn second level caching on and off.

Summary

We learned a lot in this chapter about how we can access the database through NHibernate and create, update, or delete objects in the database. We have also discussed the most basic methods of retrieving existing data from the database.

Specifically, we covered:

- What a NHibernate session is and how we use it
- Why we want to use transactions
- The session factory and how we can create one
- Managing sessions in various types of applications

Now that we've learned so much about sessions and how to access the database through a session to manipulate data, we are ready to move on and discuss (unit) testing, which will be the main topic of the next chapter.